M0025

POMPONIUS MELA

GEOGRAPHY/DE SITU ORBIS A.D.43

Translated from the Latin
by
Paul Berry

Studies in Classics
Volume 3

The Edwin Mellen Press
Lewiston•Queenston•Lampeter

Library of Congress Cataloging-in-Publication Data

This book has been registered with The Library of Congress

This is volume 3 in the continuing series
Studies in Classics
Volume 3 ISBN 0-7734-8558-9
SCl Series ISBN 0-88946-684-X

A CIP catalog record for this book is available from the British Library.

The Edwin Mellen Press   The Edwin Mellen Press
Box 450   Box 67
Lewiston, New York   Queenston, Ontario
USA 14092-0450   CANADA L0S 1L0

The Edwin Mellen Press, Ltd.
Lampeter, Ceredigion, Wales
UNITED KINGDOM SA48 8LT

Printed in the United States of America

This version of Mela's work is presented in a recollection of the kindness that was shown to the translator during an extended stay at the Vatican Library. A particular debt of gratitude is owed to Father Leonard E. Boyle, a Dominican priest, who is the Prefect of that most exquisite of rooms. By his kind allowance, a reproduction of Mela's work (the typeset edition of 1493) appears on each facing page of this version. It will be understood that the Prefect stands entirely free and clear of the shortcomings which the reader will point out in the translation.

CONTENTS

INTRODUCTION

Pomponius Mela was a Roman author who, in the early part of the 1st Century A.D., wrote the first systematic geography in Latin literature. Nothing of his life is known. It is only by a passing remark he makes (Book II, page 21), during his description of the southern coast of Spain, that we know he was born in the area of Calpe (the present day Gibraltar), "...this is the place that we are from." Biographical data on his life is otherwise entirely lacking. But with considerable confidence, historians have been able to date his geography to the year A.D. 43. Mela describes (Book III, page 12) a military expedition to Roman Britain, to be set in motion later that year. He then describes the victory celebration being planned in the Emperor's honor at the time of his triumphal return to Rome. From later Roman historians, who wrote during the 2nd Century A.D., it is known that this expedition to Britain took place in the second year of the reign of the Emperor Claudius, and the text is thereby datable to the year A.D. 43.[1]

Mela did not attempt an original work. It was based, to a great extent, on the Greek geographers who lived centuries before his time, beginning with the descriptive geography occasionally found in the epics of Homer. Mela seldom refers to them by name, but these Greek authors could be listed chronologically by the dates generally assigned to their works.

Hecataeus of Miletus	500 B.C.	*Circuit of the Earth*
Herodotus of Halicarnassus	425 B.C.	*History*
Xenophon of Athens	400 B.C.	*Anabasis*
Aristotle of Stageira	350 B.C.	*The Earth*
Eratosthenes of Cyrene	250 B.C.	*Chronographiae*
Polybius of Megapolis	150 B.C.	*History*
Strabo of Amasia	10 B.C.	*Geographica*

---

[1]Suetonius: *Lives of the Caesars*, (Claudius) 17 - 2; Dio Cassius: *Roman History*, 60 - 21 - 3

From Aristotle and the later Greeks, Mela knew the world was a sphere, and on the opening page of his geography, he divided the globe into sections of latitude and longitude. By longitude, he separated both hemispheres into their four quadrants, north, south, east and west, according to the path of the sun. By latitude, he separated the hemispheres into five horizontal zones. The upper and lower two were uninhabitable by their extreme cold, the center belt was unavailable by its heat, and the two temperate zones lying on each side of it made up the known globe. The Roman world was centered around their own sea, the Mediterranean, their *mare nostrum*. The other temperate zone was presumed to be inhabited, but little was known of it, except that its people would be required to stand with their feet opposite to the Romans, they were the *Anti-podes*.

Greeks aside, the most direct influence on Mela's work was actually a Roman living in his own day, Marcus Agrippa. A world survey had been planned during the life of Julius Caesar, but the project had not been implemented until a generation later, well into the reign of Caesar Augustus (27 B.C. - 14 A.D.). For this vast assignment, Augustus turned to this trusted Commander in Chief, Marcus Agrippa, considered by some historians to be one of the greatest of all Roman generals. The measurement of the world was to be entire - politically, topographically, demographically, strategically, economically - and no province in the Empire was to be omitted. It was to this survey that Luke made reference in his Gospel, "...In those days, there went forth a decree from Caesar Augustus that all the world should be counted" (*Luke 2:11*). Of Agrippa's census, nothing has survived; not even a fragment has remained. The loss of his record opens a most keenly felt gap in our knowledge of Roman history.

Notwithstanding, his work was in general circulation throughout the 1st Century A.D., and although Mela does not refer to Agrippa by name, the assumption is unavoidable that he relied on his work at every turn. The Roman author, Pliny the Elder, writing a generation after Mela's time, points repeatedly to the accuracy of Agrippa's survey. The confidence was well placed. One example, quoted by Pliny, might be cited. Agrippa estimated the width of Britain to be 300 miles at its base, and its length to be nearly 800 miles to the north.[2] The mileage is essentially the same as noted by a present-day tourist.

The Romans commonly employed three standards of measure, and all of them occur in Mela's work: the mile, the stadia, and the acre. The mile was considered to be 2,000 paces counted off by a Roman legion, marching at a full cadence over level terrain. Then, just as in our own day, the infantry stride approximated 31 inches, giving a total length of 62,000 inches (5,167 feet), or about a half block less than our statute mile. The method of measure was not limited to the military. Cicero described his meeting with the building contractor, Mescidius, during the planning stage of Cicero's suburban villa. The work involved the excavation of a water channel across an open stretch of ground. Side by side, they marched off the lineal distance of 3,000 paces.[3] The stadia was a one-eighth part of the Roman mile, and the stadia-rod method is a system of land measurement used by surveyors today. The Roman acre (*ager*) was considered to be the proportions of the ordinary plowed field (also called a *campus*), and its normal dimensions were given, in a casual remark made by the poet Horace, as 300 feet by 1,000 feet.[4] A standard less often used by Mela was the Roman foot. According to Vitruvius, an architect of the Classical Period, a foot was seen as one sixth of a man's height.[5]

A measuring rod to place a value on Mela's geography would seem to have been given by history itself. The survival of his book for 2,000 years is remarkable, and the toil involved in the long process was appalling. From Mela's own handwritten worksheets, the professional scribe at Rome would have copied the entire text in bold capital letters, on costly papyrus. The process would then have to be repeated, for reasons of wear, in each succeeding age. The survival of Mela's

[2] Pliny: *Natural History*, 4 - 16. Modern historians have also considered Agrippa's survey. J.J. Tierney: "The Map of Agrippa," in: *Proceedings of the Royal Irish Academy*, vol. 63, 1963, p. 151 ff.

[3] Cicero: *Letters to Quintus*, 3 - 1 - 3

[4] Horace: *Satires*, 1 - 8 - 12

[5] Vitruvius: *Architecture*, 3 - 1 - 2

work for fifteen centuries by the labor of the hand copyist (the so-called manuscript tradition) presents a complex history of its own.[6] Historians have expressed little doubt that maps would likely have accompanied the earliest manuscript copies. Maps had existed throughout Roman history; the legions would not have marched without them. The presence of maps would also serve to justify the lack of precision sometimes found in Mela's descriptions; one city is located, "...*toward the right hand*," of another, and a mountain is sited, "...*beyond an estuary*," of a river. A map to accompany the text would remove the haze from some of his observations.

Mela's book was seen in modern published form eighteen years after the invention of the movable type printing press by Johann Gutenberg in 1453. The Vatican Library holds seven printed editions of Mela's geography, which typographers have classified as *incunabula* – any book published before 1500 during the birthing stage of printing, the time of its incubation. Together, the Vatican collection, running from 1471 to 1498, offers a chronological sequence in which the evolution of the printed page may be traced to its earliest days. The problems seen in the first typeset versions: the fading of letter density near the lower lines, the occasional gaps in word spacing, the omission of punctuation, the absence of titles and superscriptions, the lack of chapter divisions, the sporadic loss of type weight, the irregular margins, the isolated ink spotting, were all gradually overcome as the era of the *incunabula* evolved.

Three edition from the *incunabula* are noteworthy. In them, the year, the city and the printer are identifed on the opening leaves: 1478, Venice (Franciscus Renner), 1482, Venice (Erhard Ratdolf) and 1493, Venice (Hermolaus Barbatus).

It is the printed text of 1493 which appears, in facsimile form, on each facing page of this translation. The text shows a generally uniform punctuation, a fairly consistent capitalization and a mainly regular system of abbreviation. Some of the more common abbreviations might be noted.

---

[6]The manuscript tradition for Mela's work has been delineated by the Italian classicist, Giuseppe Billanovich. His extended essay appeared in the journal, *AEVUM*, in February, 1956

alit	alitus	fanu	fanum	pcul	procul
alueu	alveus	fex	ferox	pdicare	praedicare
amniu	amnicus	fros	frons	perq	per quem
atra	atratus	getes	gentes	ppe	prope
aute	autem	i	id	ptes	partes
cais	canis	ide	id est	ptinax	pertinax
capos	campos	imanes	immanes	puicia	provincia
ctua	centum	isula	insula	qa	quia
citra	citerior	iteru	iterum	qnqe	quinque
coluna	columna	maxie	maxime	quide	quidem
cu	cum	mos	mons	quonda	quondam
danu	damnum	na	nam	seqt	sequitur
delubru	delubrum	naque	namque	tame	tamen
duum	duplum	nome	nomine	tatumodo	tantummodo
equis	aequalis	nume	numine	tu	tum
etia	etiam	ome	nomen	vna	variana

The shortcomings of the edition are easily demonstrated, but the perceptive reader soon realizes that the exact reverse impression is, in fact, created by a further examination of the text of 1493. The text actually stands near the entrance way of the modern printed book. Removed by only forty years from the invention of the movable type press, Mela's book offers a bold departure from Gutenberg's Latin Bible of 1453. The geography presents a case study in the transition from Gothic lettering to Italic lettering. Gone are the high twin columns of dense Gothic type, paired together like heavy pillars on each page. Mela's edition was intended for private study at the desk, rather than public reading at the lectern. The aesthetics of its typography - light, lithe, graceful, sinuous - have not been essentially bettered in five centuries.

The Latin text which has survived for 2,000 years may tell us little of Mela the author, but it casts considerable light on the Roman mind of the 1st Century A.D. The geography had not been written to enlighten provincials, that would have struck Mela as a droll idea. It was addressed to the citizens of the city, and in all the world there existed only one city. If Mela's description of Italy (Book II, page 14) would seem to be overly brief, he waves to his readers at once, "...it is known to one and all." By the same easy nod, he twice over (Book III, page 4 and Book III, page 7) dismisses, entirely unnamed, certain outlying regions with the excuse, "...they have names which no Roman would attempt to pronounce." At the same time, Mela did not fail to see the darker characteristics inherent in some provincial minds. For all their carefree existence, the natives often had no sure hold on the higher meaning of life. Their tendency toward final surrender and suicide was noted more than once (Book II, page 6; Book III, page 9, and Book III, page 15).

In direct opposition stood the Roman mind. The logic intrinsic within the Latin language seemed to produce a tendency in the reverse direction - a tidal pull toward a rationale, a motivation, a striving, a longing, a definition of the immortality of the soul. The search recurs continually in Roman literature - the philosopher, Lucretius, the orator, Cicero, the poet, Virgil. Mela was relentlessly drawn to the quest beyond the limits of any geography.

Book I, page 11
Book I, page 13
Book II, page 4
Book II, page 6
Book III, page 5

At his concluding reference, he even speaks of the search for the immortality of the soul as a flowing into the common store of human knowledge.

Whether or not Mela was a typical Roman cannot be known, the evidence is not complete. But should the assumption be made that he was 43 years of age when the geography was written, the date of his birth then becomes contemporaneous with the birth of Christ. The assumption permits no conclusion to be reached, but it does permit a composite sketch to be attempted, drawn in the reflection of the other Romans we know from Scripture.

Mela was a contemporary of the centurion who, during his tour of duty in Palestine, and free from the shackles of polytheism, built a temple to the single omnipotent God (*Luke 7:5*). Mela was of the generation of the centurion who was pointed out by Christ, "...I have not found such faith in Israel" (*Matthew 8:10*), and of the same time period as the centurion who became the first convert to Christianity at the foot of the cross

(Mark 15:39). Roman procurators were occasionally spoken of by Mela, and, regarding Pontius Pilate, Peter claimed that during the trial of Christ, "...Pilate was wont to let Him go" *(Acts 3:13)*. Peter later converted the centurion, Cornelius *(Acts 10:)*, and Paul converted the proconsul, Sergius Paulus *(Acts 13:7)*. The Roman *aedile* (treasurer) of the city of Corinth, Erastus, was a friend of Paul *(Romans 16:23)*. The Roman judge, Gallio, restored Paul's freedom to preach *(Acts 18:14)*, and the Roman tribune, Claudius Lysias, saved Paul's life *(Acts 23:27)*. Scripture tells us little of these men, but Mela's geography presents the conventional wisdom which they accepted.

Mela has but one claim to make on the modern reader's time - the fact he wrote ten years after the dawn of Christianity. To cast a light on his work is to cast a light on the time in which he lived. The world he described was common knowledge at the time of Christ, and Mela stood on the bank of the torrent when the two great rivers of history, the Word and the Empire, first began their confluence. For the reader of Roman history and the New Testament, few generations can possess a fascination so great.

       In spiritu humilitatis offertur.
          Paul Berry, 1997

Liber Primus.

Pomponii Melæ Cofmographi de fitu orbis liber primus.

Prooemium.

RBIS Situm dicere aggredior impeditum opus & facundiæ minime capax. Côftat eni fere gentium locorúq; nominibus: & eorū perplexo fatis ordine: quem perfequi longa eft magis q̃ benigna materia. Verum afpici tamen cognofciq; digniſſimum: & quod fi non ope inge nii orantis: at ipfa fui contemplatione prætium operæ at/ tendétium abfoluat. Dicam autem alias plura & exactius. Nunc autem ut quæq; erũt clariſſima & ſtrictim: ac primo qdem q̃ fit forma totius: quæ maximæ partes: quo fingulæ modo fint: utq; habitentur expediam. Deinde rurfus oras omnium & littora ut intra extraq; funt: atq; ut ea fubit ac circumluit pelagus: additis quæ in natura regionũ incola/ rumq; memoranda funt. Id quo facilius fciri poffit atq; ac cipi: paulo altius fumma repetetur.

Mundi in quattuor partes diuifio.

Mne igitur hoc quicquid eft: cui mundi cœlique nomen indidimus: unum ideft: & uno ambitu fe cunctaque amplectitur: partibus differt. Vnde fol oritur: oriens nuncupatur: aut ortus: quo demergitur: occidens uel occafus: qua decurrit: meridies. Ab aduerfa partes: feptentrio. Huic medio terra fublimis cingitur un diq; mari: eademq; in duo latera: quæ hemifphæria nomi nautur: ab oriente diuifa ad occafum zonis quinq; diftin/

THE FIRST BOOK

Pomponius Mela Cosmographer of
the situation of the World, First Book
Preface.

I set about to speak of the situation of the world, a weighty labor with little opportunity for eloquence. Being composed, indeed, almost entirely of countries and locations, it is a long and perplexing enumeration, the subject matter is greater in work than in wit. Nonetheless, one well worthy to be known and regarded. This is not for any value added by the writer himself, but for the subject itself, for those who attend to it. I shall speak elsewhere, and at greater length and exactitude. But for the present, however, I shall briefly treat that which is primary and notable in the entire whole: the plan of its larger parts, the mode of their sites and their inhabitants. Hence, these are the outer boundaries of the whole and their coastlines, within and without, according to the sea in and around them; additionally, those things native to the region and the inhabitants. To carry this attempt more easily, brief summations may be repeated.

The World Divided into Four Parts.

Everything, therefore, whether it be named heaven or earth, is one unto itself, containing itself and its amplitude within a single ambit, its parts being differentiated. That where the sun rises is called the east, where it lowers is the west, or setting, its courseway is the south. The part opposite is the north. The middle earth, being raised in elevation, is encircled east and west by the sea - itself divided on two sides called hemispheres, and these are separated into five zones, of which

1

guitur.mediã æstus infestat:frigus ultimas.Reliquæ habi
tabiles paria agunt anni tempora:uerũ nõ pariter. Antich
thones alterã:nos alterã icolimus.Illius situs ob ardorẽ in
tercedẽtis plagæ incognitus:huius dicendus est.Hæc er
go abortu porrecta ad occasum:&quia sic iacet aliquãto q̃
ubi latissima ẽ:longior ambit omnis oceano: quattuorq;
ex eo maria recipit.Vnum ab septentrione:a meridie duo
quartũ ab occasu.Suis locis illa referentur.Hoc primũ an
gustũ nec amplius decẽ milibus passuũ patens terras aperit
atq; intrat.Tũ longe lateq; diffusum abigit uaste cædentia
littora:iisdéque ex diuerso prope coeũtibus adeo i arctum
agit :ut minus mille passibus pateat.Inde se rursus:sed mo
dice admodum laxat:rursusq; ét quã fuit:arctius exit i spa
tiũ.Q̃ uo cũ est acceptũ igens iterum & magno & paludi
cæterũ exiguo ore cõiungit.Id oẽ qua uenit:quaq; dispgi
tur:uno uocabulo nostrũ mare dicit.Angustias itroituq;:
uenientis nos fretũ:græci porthmon appellãt. Q̃ ua dis
fundit alia aliis locis cognomĩa acceptat.Vbi primũ se co
arctat:hellespontus uocat.Propontis ubi expãdit:Vbi ite
rũ pressit:thracius bosphorus. Vbi iterũ effundit: pontus.
Euxinus.Q̃ ua paludi cõmittit:cimmerius bosphorus.pa
lus ipsa mæotis.Hoc mari & duobus iclytis amnibus. Ta
nai & Nilo in tres partes uniuersum diuidit . Tanais a se
ptẽtrione ad meridiẽ uergés i mediã fere mæotidã defluit
&ex diuerso Nilus i pelagus.Q̃ nod terrarum iacet a freto
ad ea flumina ab altero latere Africam uocamus:ab altero
Europẽ:ad Nilũ africã:ad Tanaï Europẽ. Vltra q̃cq̃d est

the centermost is burdened with the heat, and the other two with the cold. The remaining
two are habitable, and possess like seasons of the year, but not however, at like times.
The Antipodes - those inhabiting opposite to us - occupy one half the sphere and we the
other. Since their sector cannot be known, due to the heat in the zone between us, we must
treat, therefore, of our own situation. Hence, this extends from East to West in
orientation, lying somewhat greater in its length than its breadth. At its broadest, it fronts
the Ocean and touches upon four seas, one to the North, two at the South and one to the
West. These shall be named in their place. A particular narrow, not over ten miles wide,
leads to the mainland and penetrates it, carrying far and away, dividing the shores, yet at
either of its ends nearly joining together again - this end barely a mile across the straight.
Thereafter, however, it broadens itself again, only to enter a passage even narrower than
before. Having passed that, it flows wide again, but forming a narrow mouth enters a
basin, its current moving in the opposite direction, and flowing to either side, bears the
name Our Sea, this being the main sea. The ebb and flow of its waters at its entrance we
call the Narrows, but the Greeks call it Propontis. At the widening of its flow, however,
it takes various names in various locales. In its first constriction, it is called the
Hellespont, but at the widening again is called the Thracian Bosphorus. At full flow again
it is the Euxine Sea, and joining a lake, it is the Bosphorus of the Cimmerians, the lake
itself is the Maeotis. By this sea and by two majestic rivers, the Tanais and the Nile, the
universe is divided into three parts. The Tanais, flowing from North to South directs itself
nearly into the middle of the Maeotis; across from it, the Nile flows to the sea. The land
lying between the lake and the river is called Africa on the one side, and Europe on the
other, the Nile to Africa the Tanais to Europe. Beyond this is

Aſia eſt. Tribus hanc e ptibus tangit oceanus ita noibus ut
locis differens. Eous ab oriente. a meridie idicus. a ſeptentrione ſcythicus. Ipſa igenti ac ppetua fronte uerſa ad orientē tantū ibi ſe i latitudinem effundit: quantū Europe &
affrica. & quod iter ambas pelagus imiſſum eſt. Inde cū aliquatenus ſolida proceſſit ex illo oceano quē idicū diximᵱ
arabicū mare & perſicū: ex ſcythico caſpiū recipit: & ideo
qua recipit anguſtior. Rurſus expanditur & ſit tā lata quā
fuerat. Deinde cum iam in ſuum finem aliarumque terrarum confinia deuenit. media noſtris æquoribus excipitur
reliqua altero cornu pergit ad Nilū: altero ad Tanain. Ora
eius cum alueo Nili amnis ripis deſcendit i pelagus: & diu
ſicut illud incedit. Ita ſua littora porrigit. Deide ſit uenienti obuiam: & primum ſe ingenti ambitu incuruat. Poſt ſe
ingenti fronte ad helleſponticum fretum extendit: ab eo
iterum obliquat ad boſphorum. Iterumque ad ponticum
latus curua aditum mæotidos tranſuerſo margine attigit.
Ipſa gremio ad Tanain uſque complexa ſit ripa: qua Tanais eſt. In ea primos hominum accipimus ab oriente. In
dos & Seres & Scytas. Seres media ferme eoæ partis icolunt. Indi ultima. ambo late patentes: neque in hoc tantū
pelagus effuſi. Spectant eni ét meridiem. Indi: oráque in
dici maris: niſi ꝙ æſtus inhabitabilem efficiunt: diu continuis gentibus occupant. Spectant & ſeprétrionē Scythæ
ac littus ſcythicū. Niſi unde frigoribus arcentur: uſque ad
caſpiū ſinum poſſident. Indis proxima eſt ariacne. Deide
aria & gedroſis & perſis ad ſinū pſicū. Hūc populi pſarū

Asia. On three sides touched by the ocean, it has different names in different locations. Toward the rising of the sun, the Orient; toward the south, the Indian; toward the north, the Scythian. The landmass itself fronts the east with a latitude as great as that of Europe and Africa, along with the sea in between them. Proceeding from the ocean at full breadth, it accepts from the aforementioned Indian Ocean, as well as the Arabian, the Persian, the Scythian and the Caspian seas; where it receives them, however, it is somewhat constricted. Once again widening, it assumes its former breadth. Finally, coming to its own limit, and to the bounds of other lands, the center touches upon our own waters, and the remainder advances on the one side to the Nile and the other to the Tanais. Its mouth, with the delta of the Nile at its side, then discharges into the sea, flowing at some length in tandem. It flows at last into the sea where they meet, but forming first a great arc around. After which it carries on a broad front to the Hellespont's extended channel, and this verges toward the Bosphorus. Once again, to the side of the flow, its course transfers to the Maeotis, and touches its margin. Its volume discharges into the Tanais, and the riverine complex itself is called the Tanais. We have the understanding that these, the first men to the East are: the Indians, the Seres and the Scythians. The Seres inhabit the central tract, the Indians toward the side of the two, so far as the sea may flow to the south. The Indians also extend to the sea along with the other nations, except where it may be uninhabitable because of the heat, and so, for a long time, have occupied the whole continent. The Scythians likewise in the north extend to the Scythian Sea. Except where they are checked by the cold, they possess even to the Caspian shore. Adjacent to India is Ariana. From thence Ariana and Gedrosia and Persia lie as far as the Gulf of Persia. Inhabiting here are the people of Persia and the ambiunt.Illū alerū arabes.Ab iis:quod in africam reſtat: ætiopum eſt.Illic caſpiani ſcytis proximi ſinum caſpium cingunt.Vltra amazones:ultraꝗ eas hyperborei eſſe me morantur.Interiora terrarū multæ uariæꝗ gentes habitāt gandari:& paricani:& ba¢ri.ſuſiani pharmacotrophi.bo marei.coamani.rophanes.dahæ.Super ſcytas ſcytharūꝗ deſerta:ac ſuper caſpium ſinū Comari.Maſſegetæ.Caduīi Hircani.Hiberi:Super Amazonas & Hyperboreos Cim merii.Scythæ.Eniochoe.Georgi.Moſchi. Corſitæ. Pho riſtæ.Riphaces.atque ubi in noſtra maria tractus excedit. Mari. Antibarani: & notiora iam nomina Medi.Arme nii.Comageni.Murrani.Vegeti.Cappadoces. Gallogræ ci.Lycaöes.Phryges.Perſæ.Iſauri.Lydi.Syro cilices.Rur ſus ex iis:quæ meridiem ſpectant:eædemque gentes inte riora littora uſque ad ſinum perſicum.Sup hunc ſunt Par thi & Aſſyrii. Super illum alterum Babylonii. Et ſuper Aetiopias ægypti ripis Nili amnis & mari proximi iidem Aegiptii poſſident.Deinde arabia anguſta fronte ſequen tia littora attingit.Ab ea uſque ad flexum illū:quem ſupra rettulimus. Syria. & in ipſo flexu Cilicia.extra autē Lycia & Pamphilia.Caria.Ionia.Aeoliis.Troas uſque ad Helle ſpontum.Ab eo bithyni ſunt ad thracium boſphorū. Cir ca pontū aliquot populi alio alioꝗ ſinc.oés uno noïe pó tici dicunt̄:ad lacū Mæotici:ad tanain Sauromatæ.

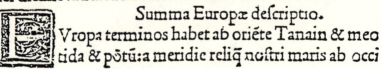

Summa Europæ deſcriptio.
Vropa terminos habet ab oriéte Tanain & meo tida & pōtū:a meridie reliꝗ noſtri maris ab occi

others of Arabia. From them, those dwelling in Africa relate to the Ethiopians. Thence after are the Caspians, by the border of the Scythians. Beyond are the Amazons, and further are the Hyperboreans. The interior land mass holds many and varied nations: the Gaudars, the Paricans, the Bactrians, the Susians, the Pharmacotrophi, the Bomarians, the Coamans, the Rophans, and the Dacians. Past the Scythians and the Scythian desert and above the Caspian Gulf are the Comars, the Massegetae, the Cadusians, the Hyrcanians, and the Hiberians. Above the Amazons and the Hyperboreans are the Cimmeranians, the Scythians, the Eniochians, the Georgians, the Moschians, the Corsitans, the Phoristans, the Riphacians as well as those who pass beyond our sea. Located here: the Mariandians, the Antibarians - now to more commonly known names - the Medes, the Armenians, the Comagenians, the Murrians, the Vegetians, the Cappadocians, the Gallogreeks, the Lycaonians, the Phrygians, the Persians, the Isaurians, the Lydians, and the Syro-Cilicians. Turning from these toward the south - these being considered as one nation - they occupy the interior even to the shore of the Persian Gulf. Here exist the Parthians and the Assyrians. Upon the other shore, are the Babylonians. Above Ethiopia, the Egyptians possess the river line of the Nile, the Egyptian waterway, as far as the sea. Thence is Arabia on a narrow front to a contact with the sea. From here to the bend spoken of before, is Syria and at the bend proper is Cilicia, and outside it, is Lycia. Pamphilia, Caria, Ionia, Aoelis, and Troas, all run from thence to the Hellespont. From it is Bithynia and the Thracian Bosphorus. Around Pontus are other peoples, with various borders - Pontians all - even to the basin of the Maeotis and to the Tanais, and to the Sarmatians.

Summary Description of Europe

Europe, has a terminus to the east at Tanais and Maeotis, with Pontus to the south and the remainder of our sea to the west.

dente Athlanticum:a septentrione britanicum oceanum.
Ora eius forma littorū Tanai ad hellespontum: qua ripa
est dictamnis: qua flexum paludis ad ponticum redigit.
Q̇ ua propontidi & hellesponto latere adiacet: contrariis
littoribus Asiæ non opposita modo:uerū etiā similis est.
Inde ad fretum nunc uaste retracta:nunc prominens tres
maximos sinus efficit:totidemq̃ in altum se magnis fron
tibus euehit.Extra fretum ad occidētem inæqualis admo⁄
dum præcipue media quæ procurrit ad septētrionem: nisi
ubi semel iterumq̃ grandi recessu abducitur: pene ut di⁄
recto limite extenta est.Mare:qd̄ primo sinu accipit Aege
um dicitur.Q̇ uod sequenti in ore Ionium.Adriaticū inte
rius.Q̇ uod ultimo nos tuscum:quod graii Tyrrhenū per
hibent.Gentium prima est Scythia alia quā dicta ē:a Ta⁄
nai media ferme pontici lateris.Hinc in ægei partē con⁄
tinens thraciæ ac macedoniæ adiungit.Tum græcia pmi
net:Aegeūq̃ ab Ionio mari dirimit.Adriatici latus Illyris
occupat.Inter ipsum adriaticum & tuscū Italia pcurrit. In
tusco intimo gallia est.Vltra hispania ē:hæc ī occidentem
deniq̃ ēt ad septentrionē diuersis frontibus uergit. Deīde
rursus gallia est longe & a nostris littoribus hucusq̃ pmis⁄
sa.Ab ea Germani.ad Sarmatas porriguntur.Illi ad Asiā.
Hæc de Europa.

Frica ab oriētis pte Nilo terminata:pelago a cæ⁄
teris:breuior ē qdē q̃ Europa:qa nec usq̃Asiæ &
nō totis huius littorib⁹obtenditͥ.Lōgior tñ ipa
q̃ latior:& qua ad fluuiū attigitͥ latissima.Vtq̃ ide pcedit.

The Atlantic Ocean has the British Ocean to the north. The mouth of this forming the shoreline from Tanais to Hellespont, and by bays and lagoons it progresses. With Propontis and Hellespont by adjacent sides, the line formed is directly opposite that of Asia, and bears a similarity to it. Hence, the flow now advancing, now retreating, forms three large inlets, all flowing toward the deep. Beyond this watercourse, to the west, is a strongly uneven coastal line, notably in the center, but in moving northward, it carries string-straight excepting for a few bays where it flows well inland. The sea advances to its first gulf, termed the Aegean. Following is the Ionian Gulf, with the Adriatic next in sequence. The last we refer to as the Tuscan, but the Greeks call it the Tyrrhenian. Regarding these countries, the first is Scythia, spoken of previously, running from Tanais near to the line of Pontus. From here the Aegean sector sits adjacent toward Thrace and Macedonia. Greece, projecting outward, divides the Aegean Sea from the Ionian Sea. By the Adriatic shoreline is Illyria. Dividing the Adriatic and the Tuscan is Italy. Inland from the Tuscan lies Gaul. Beyond that is Spain. Carrying past Spain, the landcourse runs westward and northward. Turning again, Gaul stretches past our own shoreline. From thence, bearing onward, is Germany and the Sarmatians, and these which are of Asia. This, then, pertains to Europe.

Africa is terminated on the east by the Nile and elsewhere by the sea. Not so wide as Europe, neither where it extends by the line of Asia, nor where it courses by the sea coast. It is greater in its length than its width, where it touches the riverline. From thence it proceeds

ita media præcipue in iuga exurgens pergit i curua ad oc
cafum:faftigiatque fe molliter:& ideo ex fpacio paulatim
adductor.Vbi finitur:ibi maxime angufta eft. Q uantum
incolitur eximiæ fertilis. Verū cp plæracp eius iculta:& aut
harenis fterilibus obducta:aut obfitim cœli terrarūque de
ferta funt:aut ifeftantur multo ac malefico genere anima
liū:uafta eft magis quā frequens.Mare quo cingit a feptē
trione libycū.a meridie æthiopicū. ab occidente atlanticū
dicimus.Ab ea parte:quæ libyco adiacet: pxima nilo pui
cia:quā Cyrenas uocant.Deide cui totius regionis uocabu
lo cognomen iditū eft. Africa. Cætera Numidæ & mauri
tenent.Sed maurim atlanticū pelagus expofiti.Vltra Ni
gritæ funt & pharufii:ufcp ad æthiopas.Hi & reliqua hu
ius.& totum latus:quod meridiē fpectat:ufcp i Afiæ confi
nia poffident.At fuper ea quæ libyco mari abluunt libyes
ægyptii funt:& Leucoæthiopes & natio frequens multi
plexcp getuli.Deide late uocat regio perpetuo tractu inha
bitabilis.Tum primos ab oriéte garamantas:poft augilas
& troglodytas & ultimos ad occafum atlantas audimus.
Intra fi credere libet:uix ia hoies magifcp femiferi ægypa
nes & blémyæ & gamphafantes & fatyri fine tectis paffim
ac fedibus uagi habent potius terras:q̄ habitét.Hæc fum
ma noftri orbis:hæ maxime ptes. hæ formæ gentefcp par
tium.Nunc exactius oras fitufcp dicturo ide eft cōmodif
fimū icipere:unde terras noftrū pelagus ingredit .Et ab iis
potiffimū:quæ in fluenti dextera funt.Deide ftringere lit
tora ordine:quo iacét pagratifcp oibus:q̄ mare attingunt

toward the center, rising continuously higher as it runs to the west. Mountainous particularly in the middle, this area slants westward, and where it terminates the ridgeline is more angular. Those parts which are inhabited show an extreme fertility. Yet those others being uncultivated are sterile barrens, and not farmed for reason of the drought. Many kinds of wild beasts are numerous to the area. The sea, circling to the north, touches Libya, to the south is Ethopia, that to the west we call the Atlantic. To this part lies Libya, but approximate to the Nile is that which they call Punic Cyrene. Hence, the entire region is called by the known name of Africa. The remainder, then, being Numidia and Mauritania - Mauritania extending to the Atlantic Ocean. Past this are the Nigritae with the Pharusians toward Ethopia. These, and the remainder have the entire length facing to the south, possessing even to Asia. But above these are those people who are washed by the Libyan Sea: the Libyan-Egyptians, the Lighter Ethopians and those numerous nations of the Getulians. Thence, to the side, lies a great tract which is perpetually barren. To the east are: first the Garamantians, then the Augulae and the Troglodytes and lastly, on the west, the Atlantans, as we understand. To the interior, if it is to be believed - and with difficulty - the half wild Egypanes, the Blemians, the Gamphasantes and the Satyrs. All dwelling without walls, they have no fixed seats of habitation and possess only the land. All this is the summation of our world: its major parts and the general partitions. Now, I begin to speak more exactly of the delineations and mode of the lands at that place where our sea makes its entrance toward the greater lands. Speaking particularly with regard to those which lie toward our right hand. Thence, to trace out the sea course as it lies in the order of the provinces sited toward the sea, and

legere ēt illa:quæ cingit oceanus:donec curſus icepti ope
ris intra extraꝗ circūuectus orbē illuc:unde cæpit redeat.

Particularis Aphricæ deſctiptio.

Ictum eſt atlanticū eē oceanū:ꝗ terras ab occidē
te cōtingeret.hic in noſtrū mare pgentibus læua
hiſpania.Mauritania dextera eſt.Primæ ptes illæ
Europæ hæ africæ.Eius oræ finis mulucha:caput atꝗ exor
diū ē pmontoriū:quod græci āpleuſian:afri aliter ſed idē
ſignificante uocabulo appellant.In eo ē ſpecus Herculi ſa
cer & ultra ſpecū Tinge oppidū puertus ab Anteo:ut ſerūt
cōditum.Extat rei ſignū parma elephantino tergore exe
cto ingens:& ob magnitudinem nulli nunc uſuro habilis:
quam locorū accolæ ab illo geſtatā p uero habent tradūtꝗ
& inde eximie colūt.Deinde eſt mons præaltus ei:quē ex
aduerſo hiſpania attollit obiectus: hunc abylā:illū calpen
uocāt colūnas Herculis utrūꝗ.Addit fama nois ſabulam
Herculē ipſum iūctos olim ꝑpetuo iugo diremiſſe colles:
atꝗ ita excluſum antea mole montiū oceanū:ad quæ nūc
inūdat:admiſſū.Hic iā mare latius fundit :ſūmotaſꝗ ua
ſtius terras magno ipetu iſlectit.Cæterū regio ignobilis: &
uix qcꝗ illuſtre ſortita puis oppidis habitat : parua flumia
emittit:ſolo ꝗ uiris melior:& ſegnitie gentis obſcura. Ex
iis tamen:quæ cōmemorare nō piget.Montes ſunt alti: ꝗ
continenter & quaſi de induſtria in ordinem expoſiti ob
numerum ſeptē ob ſimilitudinem fratres uocantur. Tam
uada fluuius:& ruſigada & ſiga paruæ urbes: & portus: cui
magno eſt cognomē ob ſpatiū.Mulucha ille:quē diximus

to list out those contingent upon the ocean. Turning, then, in the track of the orbit -within and without - we return again to the starting place.

Particulars of Africa described.

It has been stated that the Atlantic Ocean borders the earth to the west. At this place, those traveling into our sea have Spain to their left. Mauritania is to their right. The first is Europe, Africa the latter. At the far end of the land is the Mulucha River. At its head and limit is the Promontory, which to the Greeks is Apleusia: to the Africans it is signified by another name. In this is a cavern sacred to Hercules, and past the cavern is the city of Tinge; its foundation begun by Anteus. Existing still is an object representing the shield of elephant hide, so great in magnitude as to be, now, beyond the use of anyone. This is spoken of by the inhabitants as being carried by him as a youth, and this object they worship. From here, placed directly opposite to Spain, is a high peak called Abyla, the other called Calpe - together called the Pillars of Hercules. Attached to these names is the fable that Hercules divided these heights into two hills, permitting the sea to enter as it now flows. Here, the sea flows out widely, cutting great bays into the land by its velocity. Yet, the remainder of the region is ignoble, having nothing else illustrious about it, having villages, small rivers and a sluggish and passive population. Hence, little else need be reported. But, high mountains are present, which by order of their arrangement, being aligned in a row, are referred to as the Seven Brothers. Here is the river, Tamuada and the small towns Rusigada and Siga, and the port which, on account of its size, is called The Spacious. Mulucha, as we have said,

amnis eft igentium olim regnorũ terminus Bocchi Iugur
thæq̃. Ab eo Numidia ad ripas expofita fluminis Ampfa
gæ fpacio qdem q̃ Mauritania anguftior é. Verũ & culta
magis & ditior. Vrbiũ: quas habet maxiæ funt Cyrtha p
cul a mari: nunc Sittianorũ colonia: quondã regũ domus
Iubæ & Siphacis: cum foret opulentiffima. Iol ad mare ali
quando ignobilis. Nunc qa Iubæ regia fuit: & ǫ Cæfar ea
uocitat̃ illuftris. Citra hác: nam i medio ferme littore fita
eft. Carténa & Arfenaria funt oppida & ampfa caftellũ &
Iaturus finus & fardabale fluuius ultra monumentũ cõmu
ne regiæ gentis. Deide Icofiũ & uthifia urbes effluentes in
ter eas Ancus & Nabar: aliaq̃ quæ taceri nullũ rerũ famæ
ue difpendiũ eft. Interius & longe fatis a littore: fi fidẽ res
capit: mirũ admodũ fpinæ pifciũ: muricũ oftreorũq̃ frag
menta: faxa attrita uti folét fluctibus & nõ differétia. mari
nis ifixæ cautibus anchoræ. Alia & huiufmodi figna atque
ueftigia effufi olim ufq̃ ad ea loca pelagi i cãpis nihil alẽti
bus effe iueniriq̃ narrant̃. Regio quæ feqt̃ a pmontorio
Metagonio ad aras philenorũ pprie nomen Africæ ufur
pat. In ea funt oppida Hipporeius & Ruficade & Tabra
ca. Deide tria pmótoria: cãdidũ. Apollinis. Mercurii: uafte
piecta i altũ duos grádes finus efficiunt hipponéfem uo
cát pximũ ab hipponediarryto: qd littori eius appofitũ é.
In altero funt caftra lælia: caftra cornelia. flumen Braga
da. Vtica & Carthago: ambæ inclytæ: ambæ a phœnicibus
conditæ. Illa fato Catonis infignis. Hæc fuo nunc populi
romãi colonia: olim iperii eius ptinax æmula. Iam qdem

forms the terminus of Boccus and of Jugurtha, and these names, in days of old, stood for kingdoms. From that terminus, then, the Numidians occupy to the line of the river Ampsaga, a space more limited than that of Mauritania, but here, however, a people of greater wealth and culture. Having there the notable town of Cirta, it is sited at some distance from the sea. At present, the colonists are the Sittians, but at one time, here were the homes of the kings, Juba and Syphax, both places of great opulence. Iol, by the sea, was in former times ignoble, but it became the ruling place of Juba, and, so, is called Caesarea the Illustrious. The city, placed near the center of the seaside, has Cartena and Arsenaria as nearby cities, along with the fortress Ampsa, the bay Laturus, and the river Sardabale. At a distance, is the common burial monument of the nation's kings. Thence is Icosium and Uthisia, the cities, and flowing between them, Ancus and Nabar, the rivers, and others of no real consequence. To the interior, a great way from the shore, - if this is to be credited - are found the spines of fishes, fragments of sea creatures, stones worn smooth and not different from those rounded by waves in the sea, and anchors held fixed in the rocks. Additional things of this type and other vestiges of the sea from times past are reported to be found in the vacant barrens. Those regions lying from the promontory of Metagonius to the altars of the Phileni all appropriate the name of Africa. In it are the towns of Hipporegum, Rusicade, and Tabraca. Beyond are three promontories, these named, White, Apollo and Mercury. A vast flowing thence forms two great inlets, approximate to the shoreline: the one called Hipponesis and the other Hipponediarryto. Opposite, there are the towns of Laelia and Cornelia. Past here is the river Bragada, and the cities of Utica and Carthage, both beautiful and both founded by the Phoenicians. The last is famed for the fate which it suffered under Cato. It is colonized now by the Romans, but in former times it was an enduring stronghold in opposition to the Empire. At present restored to its former opulence,

iterũ opulẽta:et nunc tã prioꝛũ excidio reꝛũ q̃ ope præsen/
tium clarior Hadrumẽtum.Leptis.Clupea. Abꝛotonum:
Taphiæ.Neapolĩs hinc ad ſyrti adiacent:ut iter ignobilia
celeberrimæ Syrti ſinus eſt cẽtũ fere milia paſſuũ:qua ma/
re accipit patẽs;trecẽta:qua cingit̃.Verũ iportuoſus atque
atrox:& ob uadoꝛũ frequentiũ breuia magiſꝗ ẽt ob alter
nos motus pelagi affluentis & refluentis ifeſtus.Super hũc
ingens palus amnem Tritona recipit.ipſa Tritonis.Vnde
& Mineruæ cognomen inditum eſt:ut incolæ arbitrantur
ibi genitæ.faciuntꝗ ei ſabulæ aliquam fidem:ꝗ quem na
talem eius putant:ludicris uirginum iter ſe decertantium
celebrãt.Vltra eſt Oea oppidum & Cinyps fluuius p uber/
rima arua decidens.Tũ leptis altera & ſyrtis nomine atꝗ
igenio par priori.Cæterum altero fere ſpatio qua dehiſcit
quaque flexum agit amplior.Eius pmontoriũ eſt Boꝛion
ab eoꝗ icipiens oꝛa:quã Lotophagi tenuiſſe dicuntur uſꝗ
ad phycũta:& id pmontoriũ é iportuoſo littore ptinax
Aræ ipſe nomen ex philenis fratribus traxere: qui contra
cyrenicos miſſi Carthagine ad dirimẽdum cõditione bel/
lũ diu iã de finibus & cũ magnis amboꝛũ cladibus geſtũ
Poſtquã i eo qd cõuenerat nõ manebat :ut ibi legati cõcur
rerant certo'tẽpore utrinꝗ dimiſſi ibi termini ſtatuerẽtur:
pacti de itegro ut qcqd citra eẽt popularibus cederet.Mirũ
& memoria digniſſimũ facinus hic ſe uiuos obrui ptule/
rũt.Inde ad catabatmõ cyrenaica puicia é:i eaꝗ ſũt Ham
monis oraculũ fidei iclytæ:& froñs quẽ ſolis appellant &
rupes qdã auſtro ſacra.Hæc cũ hominũ manu attingitur:

it is now widely remembered for its previous destruction, more so than for its present eminence. From here is Hadrumentum, Leptis, Culpes, Abrotonum, Taphiae and Naples, and all these, along the famed Syrtis sandbank, are of little note. Syrtis, where it opens toward the sea, the shore courses along nearly a hundred miles, but it effects a radius of three hundred miles. Indeed, it is impassable here and unyielding for reason of the shallows and the flat narrows, and the alternating ebb and flow of the sea. Beyond this is a great sea marsh, accepting the river Triton, and so itself is called Tritonis. Here the name Minerva is used; the dwellers suppose that she was born there. This fable they offer as a truth, and maintain a course for the celebration of contests among virgins. Beyond is the city, Oea and the stream Cinyps which flows through this fruitful area. Then is the alternative Leptis and Syrtis, in names similar to the former, but these greater in size than the others. Near this is the promontory, Borion, and from it, the beginning of the bay: this, it is claimed, had been held by the Lotophagi (the Lotus Eaters) even so far as Phycunta. Here is the promontory projecting from the shoreline as a stronghold. The altars there are named after the brothers Philenii. These, having been sent from Carthage against the Cyrenians to make an end of that long war over their borderlines, they produced a great toll on both sides. Thereafter, the covenant was not maintained as understood, therefore that place where their two legates should meet would establish the border. Marvelous and memorable was this pact made by those two who were buried alive at the place. Proceeding from here, then, is Catabathmos in the province of Cyrene. Here are the oracles of Hammon, admirable for their fidelity, along with the fountain called the Cliff of the Sun, which is held sacred, as it regards the South wind. This, should it be touched by the hand of man,

ille imodicus exurgit:harenasq; quasi maria agens sic sæ╱
uit:ut æquor fluctib⁹ fons media nocte feruet:mos & pau
latim tepescens fit luce frigidus:tunc ut sol surgit ita frigi╱
dior:subinde p meridié maxie riget: Sumit deide tepores
iteru & prima nocte calidus:atq; ut illa pcedit:ita calidior
rursus cu est media pferuet.In littora pmotoria sut zephy
rion: & naustathmos:portus paretonius.Vrbes Hesperia
Apollonia.Ptolemais.Arsinoe.atq; unde terris nomé est
ipsa Cyrene:Catabathmos uallis deuexa in ægyptum finit
aphricá.Ore sic habitant ad nostru maxime ritu moratis
cultoribus:nisi ꝙ quidam linguis differunt: & cultu deoru
quos patrios seruant:ac patrio more uenerantur.Proximis
nullæ quidem urbes stant:tamen domicilia sunt:quæ Ma╱
palia appellantur:uictus asper & mundiciis carens. Primo
res sagis uelant᷄: uulgus bestiaru pecuduq; pellibus: humi
quies epulæq; capiunt . Vasa ligno fiunt aut cortice:potus
est lac succusq; baccaru:cibus est caro plurimu ferina. Na
gregibus qa id solu optimu est:quoad pot pcit .Interiores
ét in cultius:sequunt᷄ uagi pecora:utq; a pabulo ducta sut:
ita se ac tuguria sua promouent atq; ubi dies deficit:ibi no
ctem agut:quáꝙ i familias passim & sine lege dipsi:nihil i
comune consultant:tamen quia singulis aliquot simul có
iuges:& plures ob id liberi agnatiq; sunt nusquá pauci. Ex
his q ultra deserta esse memorant .Atlátes solem execran╱
tur:& dum oritur & dum occidit ut ipsis agrisq; pestiferu.
Nomina singuli non habent:non uescuntur animalibus
neq; illis inꝗete qualia cæteris mortalibus uisere dat . Tro

stirs up an immoderate surge through the sand as though it were being agitated by the sea, and has a flowing motion similar to water. The fountain, in the middle of the night, is boiling hot, however, by degrees, it becomes tepid, and by daybreak is cool. At sunrise it turns colder, and at the noontime meridian becomes nearly frozen. Thereafter it becomes tepid again, and at early nightfall becomes warm. Further in the advancing night, it reverts to hot again, as before. By the shoreline are the promontories Zephyrion and Naustathmos and the port Paretonius. Thence are the cities, Hesperia, Apollonia, Ptolemais, Arsinoe, and these are all within the land named Cyrene proper. Catabathmos, a valley which inclines toward Egypt, forms the border of Africa. And thus it is that the shoreline is inhabited, for the most part by those similar to us in ways and culture, except for certain ones who differ in language. Others differ in the cult of the gods, venerating those according to the custom of the country. None of the cities stand in close proximity, and the houses are referred to as Mapalia (the settlements). Their victuals are hard, and are lacking in sanitation. Those who are foremost among them cover themselves in mantles; the commoners go about in the hides of beasts. They eat upon the earth of the ground, and they sleep there. Their vessels are wooden or bark, and they drink milk or the juice of berries. Their meat is that of various wild beasts - but not the domesticated herds - for these are their prized possessions. Those at the interior, follow the wandering flocks to different pastures, and move their camps by day, and remain in them at night. Wherefore, the families are scattered through the households, without customary law, for they do not gather as a normal commune. Each possesses wives in cohabitation, relatives are many, and groups are numerous. Those people beyond the desert are the Atlates, who blaspheme the sun at its rising and its setting as a curse to their agriculture. They do not have individual names, nor do they eat of living animals. Nor, is it given to them to see, in times of quiet, the things seen by other mortals.

glodytæ nullarum opum domini ſtrident magis q̃ loquũ
tur:ſpecus ſubeunt alunturq; ſerpentibus.Apud garaman,
tas ēt armenta ſunt ea:quæ obliqua ceruice paſcunt.Nam
pronis directa in humũ cornua officiunt.Nulli certa uxor
eſt.Ex his q̃ tam confuſo parentum coitu paſſim incertiq;
naſcuntur:quos p ſuis colant:formæ ſimilitudine agno,
ſcunt.Augilæ manes tantũ deos putant:p eos deierāt: eos
ut oracula cōſulũt:præcatiq; quæ uolũt:ubi tumulis icubue
re: p reſponſis ferũt ſomnia.Fœminis eorũ ſoléne eſt no
cte:qua nubunt:omniũ ſtupro patere:q̃ cũ munere adue,
nerint:& tũ cũ plurimis cōcubuiſſe maximũ decus:in reli,
quũ pudicitia iſignis eſt.Nudi ſunt Gamphaſantes: armo
rũq; oĩum ignari:nec uitare ſciunt tela nec iacere: ideoque
obuios fugiũt:neq; aliorũ q̃ q̃bus idem igenii ē:aut cōgreſ
ſus aut colloqa patiunt.Blēmys capita abſunt:uultus i pe
ctore eſt. Satyris præter effigié nihil humani. Aegypanu
quæ celebrat ea forma eſt.Hæc de Aphrica.

        Aſiæ deſcriptio particularis.

Syæ prima pars ægyptus iter catabathmō & ara
bas ab hoc littore penit9 imiſſa donec æthiopiã
dorſo cōtingat .ad meridié refugit terra expers
imbriũ mire tñ fertilis:& hominũ aliorũq; aialiũ pſæcun
da generatrix.Nilus efficit amniũ i noſtrorũ mare pmean
tiũ maximus.Hic ex deſertis africæ miſſus nec ſtati nauiga
ri facilis:nec ſtati nilus ē:& cũ diu ſimplex ſæuuſq; deſcen
dit:circa Meroen late patenté iſulā in æthiopiã diffundit:
alteraq; ex parte aſtaboras altera aſtapus dictus eſt: ubi rur

The Troglodytes, owning no domestic goods, can only hiss and squeak in their speaking; they occupy caverns below the ground, and live on serpents. Regarding the Garmantes and their cattle - the beasts graze in pastures with their necks held askew at an oblique angle, for their horns grow pointing down toward the ground. None of the inhabitants has a wife to himself. From this results a confusion of parentage, with casual unions producing a mixed lineage. They know themselves only from a similarity to some nearby kin. The Augilans suppose the gods to be the spirits of the dead; they make vows to them and consult them as oracles. They pray to them, after which they recline on their graves, and, in the repose of sleep, accept their response. A solemn custom is held among the women, that during the marriage night the woman will accept the usage of any and every man who approaches with some remuneration. This is seen as great decorum, but afterward they remain entirely chaste. The Gamphasantes go about nude and have always been lacking in any knowledge of arms; neither able to flee from the arrow nor to use it. Wherefore, their course is to fly from everyone except those of their own tribe, and they do not congregate with others. The Blemians seem to be without heads; their faces are near the breastbone. The Satyrs have only the effigy of humans, for they lack humanity itself. The Egyptians, however, are widely famed, and they are admirable. These things, then, pertain to Africa.

Particulars of Asia Described.

Asia, at its primary part, is Egypt which is between Catabathmos and Arabia, and extends southward even to the area of Ethiopia. The south here experiences no rainfall, however the land is fertile and is actually a fruitful generator for both man and beast. The Nile has produced this riverine condition, and of all the streams flowing into our sea, it is the greatest. This river, flowing out of the deserts of Africa, is not entirely navigable, nor is it everywhere called the Nile. It runs at considerable length as a single course, but around the broad island of Meroe, in Ethiopia, it divides, with Astaboras on one side and Astapos on the other.

fus coit:ibi nomen hoc capit.Inde partí afper ptim naui/
gia patiés in imané lacú deuenit:ex quo præcipiti impetu
egreſſus & Tachépſo alterá inſulam amplexus uſqʒ ad ele/
phantidé urbé ægyptiam atrox adhuc feruenſqʒ decurrit.
Tum demú placidior:& iá pene nauigabilis: primú iuxta
certas orú oppidú triplex eſſe icipit.Deíde iterumqʒ diui/
ſus ad Delta & ad Metilin it p omné ægyptum uagus atqʒ
diſperſus:ſeptéqʒ i oras es ſcídés ſingulis tamé grádis euol
uitur.Non pererrat aút tantú eam:ſed æſtiuo ſydere exun
dans ét irrigat:adeo efficacibus aquis ad generandú alen/
dumqʒ ut.præter id qpſcatet piſcibus:qʒ hippopotamos cro
codiloſque uaſtas belluas gignit:glebis ét iſundat animas
ex ipſaque humo uitalia effingat:hoc eo máifeſtú é qʒ ubi
ſedauit diluuia:ac ſe ſibi reddidit:per humétes cápos quæ
dam nondum pſecta animalia:ſed tum primum accipien
tia ſpiritum:& ex parte iam formata:ex parte adhuc terrea
uiſuntur.Creſcit porro:ſiue qp ſolute magnis æſtibus niues
ex immanibus æthiopiæ iugis largius quá ripis accipi que/
ant defluunt:ſiue qp ſol hyeme terris propior:& ob id ſon
tem eius minuens tunc altius abit:ſinitque integrum: & ut
eſt pleniſſimus ſurgere:ſiue qp p ea tempora flátes etheſiæ
aut actas a ſeptétrione i meridié nubes ſup principia eius
íbre precipitat:aut uenienti obuiæ aduerſo ſpiritu curſum
deſcendentis impediunt: aut harenis: quas cum fluctibus
littori applicant:hoſtia obducunt ſitqʒ maior uel qp nihil
ex ſemet ámittit:uel qp pluſq̃ ſolet accipit uel qp minus quá
debet emittit:qp ſi é alter orbis ſuntqʒ oppoſiti nobis a me

Where it joins into one stream again it is known by its one name. From here it flows in some places as a fast narrows, but in other places as a navigable stream. Then it devolves into an immense lake, and, with its impetuous flow, it surrounds the island, Tachepso, and from there runs forcefully to Elephantine, an Egyptian city. Afterward, it becomes more placid, and, nearly navigable, directs itself to the town limits of Cerealis, branching here into three parts. Thence, dividing itself further at the Delta around Metilis, and finally cutting itself into seven streams, all flowing strongly out of Egypt, it falls at last into the sea. It washes not only though its own territory - the torrent of the summer which irrigates all - but also plentifully bears many types of fish, and among these are the hippopotamus and the crocodile. These are gigantic and warlike beasts which can infuse life into the very clods of the earth, and generate a like type. These are completely manifest when they are in a swarm, and then return to the stream. But then, when in spawn on the bankside, they seem partly to be in life and partly yet in the incipient stage, and resemble the ground itself. Regarding the cresting of the stream - either because of the great heat, or because of the melting snows coursing down from the heights of Ethiopia cause the river channel to overflow and later in summer to rise to the full crested height, or possibly because the northerly trade winds yearly drive the clouds to the south and thereby lessen the solar effects by their offsetting winds and their moderating currents - all of these things produce the end result of a great deposit of sand at the shoreline. This joins, then, with the sandbank already at the seaside, losing nothing, but ever increasing the overall deposit. If it should be that there is another orbit which is positioned opposite to us in the south,

ridie Antichthones:ne illud qdem a uero nimium abſceſ
ſerit:in illis terris ortum amnē:ubi ſubter maria cæco al
ueo penetrauerit:in noſtris rurſus emergere: & hac re ſol
ſtitio accreſcere:cp tum hyems ſit: unde oritur. Alia quocp
in his terris mira ſunt.In quodam lacuchemnis iſula lucos
ſiluaſcp & Apollinis grande ſuſtinens templum natat: &
quocūcp uenti agunt pellitur.Pyramides tricenum pedum
lapidibus extructæ:quarū maxima:tres nācp ſunt: quattu
or fere ſoli iugera:quæſedem occupat totidem in altitudi
nem erigitur.Moeris aliquando campus nunc lacus uigin
ti milia paſſuum in circuitu patens:altior q̃ ad nauigandū
magnis onuſtiſcp nauibus ſatis ē.Pſammetichi opus labi
rynthus domos mille & regias duodecim ppetuo parietis
ambitu amplexus marmore extructus ac tectus unum in ſe
deſcenſum habet.Intus pene inumerabiles uias multis am
bagibus huc & illuc remeantibus:ſed continuo anfractu &
ſæpe renocatis porticibus ancipites qbus ſubinde alium ſu
per alios orbem agentibus & ſubinde tantum redeunte fle
xu quantū pceſſerat:magno & inexplicabili tamen errore
pplexus eſt.Cultores regionū multo aliter a cæteris agunt.
Mortuos ſimo obliti plāgunt:nec cremare aut ſodere ſas
putant:uerū arte medicatos intra penetralia collocāt. Suis
litteris puerſe utunt:lutum iter manus farinā calcibus ſu
bigunt.Forū ac negocia fœmininæ:uiri pēſa ac domos cu
rant onera illæ humeris. Hi capitibus accipiūt parentes cū
egēt illis neceſſe ē:his librū eſt alere:cibos palā & extra ſua
tecta capiūt: obſcœna intimis ædiū reddūt:colūt effigies

it would be the Antipodes. While perhaps not standing perfectly opposite to us with regard to their orbit of the world - nonetheless their river systems appear to pass through the hidden caverns of the sea and then emerge into our own world. These show a cresting in their movement, inasmuch as the wintertime to them is the summertime to us. This and other marvels exist in that orbit of the world. Within a particular lake is found the wooded island of Chemnis which contains a great temple to Apollo, which is able to float, and is able to revolve according to the force of the winds. There are pyramids, some bearing stones thirty fee square, and of these all, three pyramids are considered to be the greatest. Each of these three covers a space of nearly four acres along the groundline, and about the same dimension in their total height. Lake Moeris is sometimes a dry flat and is sometimes at full crest, being, at that time, twenty miles in circumference. Its depth can then accept the draft of any loaded ship. Psammetichus, by much labor, built a labyrinth consisting of a thousand domiciles and twelve palaces. All this was done within a single ambit and executed in marble, even to the roofline, yet it had only one descent into it. The interior contained almost innumerable passages and return baffles either one way or the other, with reverse portals, each turning to a level below, but returning again to the beginning, so that one could not fathom a way out of it. Those living in the kingdom behave in a manner different from the accepted norm. In lamentation for the dead they daub themselves with mire. They neither burn nor bury by any ritual, but by the use of a penetrating medicine they preserve the dead in private, and childish letters are then written to them. They mix a lute cement with their hands, and tread on a grain cereal of farina with their feet. Legal questions are negotiated by the women; the men, however, engage in weaving and have charge of the home. Women bear their burdens on the shoulder, the men carry burdens on the head. Should the parents fall into a condition of need and want, they are bound to assist. Food is taken outside the walls of the house, but they return to the interior for personal needs. They worship the effigies

multorum animaliū atqʒ ipſa magis animalia ſed alii alia:
adeo ut quædam eorum ẽt per imprudẽtiam interemiſſe
capitale ſit:& ubi morbo aut forte extincta ſint:ſepelire ac
lugere ſolenne ſit.Apis populorum omnium numẽ eſt.
Bos niger certis maculis inſignis: & cauda linguaqʒ diſſi
milis aliorū:raro naſciť nec coitu pecoris:ut aiunt:ſed di
uinitus & cœleſti igne conceptus:dieſqʒ quo gigniť genti
maxime feſtus eſt.Ipſi uetuſtiſſimi:ut prædicant: hominū
trecentos & triginta reges ante Amaſim:& ſupra tredecim
miliuɯ annorum ætates certis annalibus referunt:man
datumqʒ litteris ſeruãt:dum ægyptii ſunt quater curſus ſu
os uertiſſe ſydera:ac ſolem bis iam occidiſſe:unde nũc ori
tur:uiginti milia urbiū Amaſi regnante habitarunt:& nũc
multas habitant. Earum clariſſimæ procul a mari. Says.
Memphys.Syene.Bubaſtis.Elephantin. & Thebæ utiqʒ:
ut Homero dictum eſt cẽtum portas:ſiue ut alii aiunt:cen
tum aulas habẽt: totidem olim principū domos:ſolitaſqʒ
ſingulas ubi negociorum exegerat.dena armatorum milia
effundere.In littore Alexandria Africæ contermina.Pelu
ſium arabiæ ipſas oras ſecat.Canopicum. Volbiticum.Se
ueniticum.Pathmiticum.Mendeſiū.Taniticum. Peluſia
cum nili hoſtia.

Rabia hinc ad rubrum mare ptinet:ſed illic ma
gis læta & ditior:thure atqʒodoribus abũdat.hic
niſi qua Caſio mõte attolliť:plana & ſterilis por
tum admittit Azotū ſuarū merciū ẽporiū.Quai altū abit
ado edita ut ex ſũmo uertice a q̄rta uigilia ortū ſolis oñdat

of various animals, and in certain cases, the animal itself, but some do otherwise. Should a given beast be slain, even by imprudence, it would be a capital offence. On their death, either by sickness or accident, they are buried and lamented. Apis is the most popular of the deities; a black bull with spotted markings and certainly unlike others of his type from tongue to tail. The animal is unique in the breed, and is held to have been born in a great fire from the highest heaven, and thus its birth is venerated by the people. These men claim that, in their history, three hundred and thirty kings reigned before the time of Amasis, and their chronicles indicate a continuum of thirteen thousand years. This appears in their datum list which they strictly keep, and this shows four occasions in Egypt on which the stars altered in their course and, twice over, the sun rose in the place where it now sets. During the reign of Amasis, the kingdom contained twenty thousand cities, and yet they now still have a great many. These cities are notable, but are far from the sea: Says, Memphis, Syene, Bubatis, Elephantine and Thebes. The last of these cities, Thebes, was said, by Homer, to have had a hundred gates, and others have said that it also had a hundred palaces - a mansion for each of the princes. These all had, according to the exigencies of the time, ten thousand men under arms. On the seacoast, Alexandria marks the terminus of Africa, and the city of Pelusium marks the division with Arabia. Canopicum, Volbiticum, Seveniticum, Pathmiticum, Mendesium, Taniticum and Pelusium mark the delta of the Nile.

Arabia, from this point, extends to the Red Sea. In it is to be found a place of happiness and plenty, a place of incense and aroma. There, except where Mount Casius rises toward its height, it is sterile and flat. There is, by the city of Azotus, a port of merchandise and shipping. Where the elevation here rises to its highest summit, the rising of the sun is noted at the time of the fourth vigil.

Yria late littora tenet terraſque ẽt latius ìtrorſus
aliis aliiſcꝗ nũcupata noìbus:nã & cœle diciť. &
meſopotamia & damaſcene & adiabene & ba
bylonia & iudea & ſophone:Hinc paleſtina ẽ ꝗ̃ tãgit ara
bas cũ phœnice & ubi ſe ciciliæ cõmittit.Antiochia oli ac
diu potés.Sed cũ eã regno Semiramis tenuit lõge poten⸗
tiſſima.opibus certe eius iſignia multa ſunt:duo maxie ex⸗
cellũt cõſtituta urbs miræ magnitudinis babylon.ac ſiccis
oli regionibus Euphrates & Tygris imiſſi.Cæterũ i palæ
ſtina ẽ ìgens & munita admodũ Gaza:ſic Perſæ ærariũ uo
cant & ide nomé eſt:cꝗ cũ Cambyſes armis ægyptũ pete⸗
ret:huc belli & opes & pecuniam ìtulerat. Eſt non minor
Aſcalon.Eſt Iope ante diluuium:ut ferunt cõdita ubi Ce
phea regnaſſe eo ſigno accolæ affirmant:cꝗ titulũ eius fra
triſꝗ hpineis:ueteres quædã aræ cũ religione plurima reti
nent:qn ét rei celebratæ carminibus ac fabulis ſeruatæcꝗ a
PerſeoAndromedæ clarum ueſtigium belluæ marinæ oſſa
immania oſtentant.

Hœnicen illuſtrauere phœnices ſolers hìum ge
nus & ad belli paciſcꝗ munia eximium:litteras &
litterarũ opas aliaſcꝗ ét artes maria nauibus adi⸗
re.claſſe cõfligere ìperitare gẽtibus regnũ præliũcꝗ cõméti
In ea eſt Tyros aliquando iſula nunc annexa terris deficit
cꝗ ab ìpugnante quondam Alexandro iacta opera uici te⸗
nent ulteriora.Et adhuc opulenta Sidon antequã a perſis
capereť maritimarũ urbiũ maxima.Ab ea ad pmontoriũ
euproſopon duo ſunt oppida Byblos & Botrys:ultra tria

Syria, holding the land by the seashore, as well as far to the interior, is known as Caele, and Mesopotamia, and Damascene, and Adiabene, and Babylonia, but also Judea and Sophone. Here, in addition, is Palestine, where it comes upon Arabia and Phoenicia where it is contingent to Cilicia. Antioch, in times of old, possessed greatness, and this was under the reign of Queen Semiramis. Her notable works exist yet, two great ones in particular: the marvels of the great city of Babylon, and the canal cutting the region of the Tigris and Euphrates. Otherwise, Palestine has only one fortified stronghold, located at Gaza. The Persians, however, call this Aerarium (the Treasury). It is so named after Cambyses, whose armies entered Egypt. Before the battle, he placed his riches and his wealth there. Not at all less than this is Ascalon, but it was called Iope before being flooded in the deluge. Buildings here are said, by the inhabitants, to have been built by Cepheus. The account is probable. Altars there of great age and religious significance carry his inscription, and that of his brother, Phineus. These are also celebrated in songs and fables, including legends of the rescue of Andromeda by Perseus. They produce in addition, the evidence of the bones of the great sea monster.

Phoenicia is made illustrious mainly through the Phoenicians themselves. Their achievements are great, whether in war or peace, whether in literature or art, whether by ships on the sea or by the administration of nations. With a fleet to impose command over the peoples, they established rule through battle. Here is Tyre, sometimes standing as an island, sometimes connected with the shore. It fell in battle to its neighbors when the outer walls were thrown down by Alexander in battle. At some distance is opulent Sidon, richest of the maritime cities before it was captured by the Persians. From here toward the promontory of Euprosopon are the two cities, Byblos and Botrys, and another three

fuerũt singulis iter se stadiis distantia:locus ex numero tri
polis dicit̃.Tum simyra castellũ:& urbs nó obscura mara
thos.Inde iã nó obliqua pelago:sed aduersa adiacēs a ter
ra grãdē sinũ i flexo tractu littoris accipit.populi dites cir
cũsidēt.situs efficit:qa regio fertilis crebris & nauigabilis
alucis flumĩnũ puia diuersas'opes maris atq; terrarũ facili
cõmercio pmutat ac miscet.In eo prima ē reliqua ps syriæ
cui antiochiæ cognomē addit̃:& i ora eius urbes Seleutia
Paltos.berytos.laudicca.arados.amnesq; inter eas eunt li
chos & hyppatos & orrontes.Tum mons amanus: & ab
eo statim myriãdros & cilices.   At i recessu ítimo locus
est magna aliquãdo discriminis fusorũ ab Alexãdro psarũ
fugientisq; Darii spectator ac testis.Nunc ne minima qdē
tunc igenti urbe celebris Issos fuit:& hac re sinus issicus di
cit̃ pcul ide Amanoides pmontoriũ iter pyramũ cydnũq;
fluuios iacet.Pyramus isso prior mallon præterfluit.Cyd
nus ultra p tarsum exit.Deide urbs ē oli arhodiis:argiuisq;
post piratis Pópeio assignãte possessa.nunc pópeiopolis.
tunc Soloe.Iuxta i puo tumulo Arati poetæ monumentũ
ideo referendũ:qa ignotũ quã ob cãm iacta in id saxa dis
siliũt.Non lõge hic corycos oppidũ portu saloq; incingit
angusto tergore continenti adnexũ.Supra specus est ñoíe
Corycius singulari igenio ac supra q̃ ut describi facile pos
sit:eximius.Grãdi nãq; hiatu patēs mõtē littori appositũ
& decē stadiorũ cliuo satis arduũ ex sũmo stati uertice apit
Tunc alte demissus & quantũ demittit̃ amplior uiret lucis
pubētibus undiq; & totũ se nemoroso laterũ orbe comple

beyond them; each having only an eighth mile (stadia) between them, and therefore called Tripolis. Next is the city of Simyra, and, not to be passed, the city of Marathos. From here not any oblique is formed with the sea, but the site is square adjacent to it, and is graded into the curve of a large inlet by the shoreline. The population around it is wealthy. The area is richly fertile, and the navigable waterways are able to accept shipping to facilitate trade and commerce, either by land or sea. Within this area is Syria, to which the name Antioch is attached, along with those of Seleucia, Paltos, Berytos, Laudicea and Arados. The rivers between them are the Lichos, the Hyppatos and the Orontes. Then is Mount Amanus, directly from it is Myriadros and Cilicia. At its deeper recess is a location of renown, famous at one time for the witness of a deception by Alexander of the fleeing Persians under Darius. Now it is quite insignificant, but was formerly famed as the city of Issos. At a great distance is the promontory Amanoides at the rivers Pyramus and Cydnus. Pyramus is nearer to Issos, and flows by Mallon. Cydnus courses beyond this and is near Tarsus. Thence, is a city, at one time held by the Rhodians, and the Argives, but after the time of Pompey it was held by pirates. It is called Pompeiopolis, but formerly was Soloe. Nearby, placed on a low hill, is the tomb of the poet Aratus, worthy of note, however obscure, because any stones which are cast there seem to fly apart. Not far from it is the city of Corycius, a saltwater port, connected to the mainland by a narrow spit. The cavern Corycius is attractive almost beyond description; it is graded toward a wide channel at the sealine, and from the elevation, it inclines to the water for a full length of about ten stadia. Then the depth falls, and drops yet again, all of it being ringed about by the hue of fresh greenery. It seems to be, on each side, an entirely sylvan grove.

eſt adeo mirificus ac pulcher:ut mētes accedentiū primo
aſpectu conſternat:ubi cōrēplati durauere nō ſaciat. Vnus
in eum deſcenſus eſt anguſtus aſper quingētorum & mil/
le paſſuum per amœnas umbras & opaca ſiluæ quiddam
agreſte reſonantis riuis hinc atꝗ illinc fluitantibus. Vbi ad
ima peruentum eſt:rurſus ſpecus alter aperitur ob alia dicē
dus. Terret ingredientes ſonitu cymbalorum diuinitus &
magno fragore crepitantiū. Deinde aliquandiu pſpicuus
mox &quo magis ſubitur:obſcurior ducit auſos penitus al
taꝗ quaſi cuniculo amittit. Ibi igens amnis ingenti frōte
ſe extollens tantummodo ſe oſtendit:& ubi magnū ipetū
breui alueo traxit:iterū demerſus abſcondit. Intra ſpaciū
eſt magis ꝗ ut pgredi qſquā auſit horribile & ideo icogni
tum. Totus aūt āguſtus & uere ſacer:habitariꝗ a diis & di
gnus & creditus:nihil non uenerabile & quaſi cum aliquo
numine ſe oſtentat. Alius ultra ē:quē typhoneū uocāt ore
anguſto & multum:ut expti tradidere:preſſus & ob id aſſi
dua nocte ſuffuſus neꝗ unꝗ pſpici facilis:ſed qa aliquādo
cubile typhonis fuit:& qa nunc demiſſa i ſe confeſti exani
mat natura fabulaꝗ memorandus. Duo deīde pmontoria
ſunt Sarpedon finis aliquādo regni ſarpedonis:& quod ci
liciā a pāphilia diſtinguit.anemuriū:interꝗ ea Celenderis
& natidos ſamiorū colōiæ ſed celēderis Sarpedoni ppior.
In pāphilia ē melas nauigabilis fluuius:oppidū Sida & al/
ter fluuius Eurymedō. Magna apud eū Cymonis atheniē
ſiū ducis aduerſus phœnicas & Perſas naualis pugna atque
uictoria fuit. Mare:quo pugnatū eſt:ex edito admodū col

It is marvelous and beauteous to all. It is a long held memory at the initial sighting, and its aura creates a lasting impression. Only one way descends into the interior, quite narrow, and about a mile and five hundred paces in length, which courses along through a most pleasant location of light and shade, with the sounds of running water about. At the bottom is another cavern, notable in certain respects. Those entering are made fearful on account of a sound as of the clash of cymbals and as of the vibration of breakage. Afterward, for a certain space, there follows a great quiet, but for those daring to proceed, the interior is nearly as dark as a mine. Thereupon, a great river flows on a broad front, but then it is choked into a narrow channel; it again submerges itself below the surface. Within this is a void, quite horrible, which therefore remains unknown. This whole space, in fact, is revered and is entirely sacred. It is held as consecrated to the gods by the inhabitants, and is dedicated to the sublime. Yet another such the like is found beyond here, the narrow mouthed Typhon cavern, spoken of by many, but, because of its obscure entrance, it is not at all easy of access for the lack of light. At one time it was the lair of the giant Typhon, but now seems only to receive whatever is lowered into it, and to that extent, is worthy of remark. From here are found two promontories: Sarpedon, which had once marked the boundary place for King Sarpedon, and then - dividing Cilicia from Pamphilia - is Anemurium, but actually in the area of Celenderis and Sarpedon. In Pamphilia is the Melas, a navigable river, and the city of Sida with another river, the Eurymedon. It was here the Athenian general, Cimon, fought against the Persians and the Phoenicians in a great sea battle, and was victorious. By the sea, where the battle was fought, rises a prominent hill;

se pspectat aspendos:quã argiui cõdiderant possedere fi
nitimi:Deinde alii duo ualidissimi fluuii œstros & catera
ctes:œstros nauigari facilis:hic qa se præcipitat ita dictus:
Inter eos Perga est oppidũ:& dianæ quã ab oppido pgeã
uocant téplum.Trans eosdé mõs sardemisos & phaselis
a mopso cõdita finis pãphilæ.Lycia cõtinuo cognomíata
a Lyco rege pandionis filio:atq ut ferunt:isestata oli chy
meræ ignibus Sydæ portu & tauri pmontorio grandé si
nũ claudit.Taurus ipse ab eois littoribus exurgens uaste sa
tis attollit.Deide dextro latere ad septétrioné:siniftro ad
meridiem uersus it i occidété rectus & ppetuo iugo:ma
gnarũq gétiũ qua dorsum agit:terminus:ubi terras diri
mit:exit in pelagus.Idé aũt & totus ut dictus est:dicitur ét
qua spectat oriétem.Deide hæmodes & caucasus & paro
pamisus.Tum caspiæ pilæ.Niphates & armeniæ pilæ:&
ubi iam nostra maria cõtigit taurus iterũ.Post eius ,pmon
toriũ flumé est lymira:& eodé nomine ciuitas:atq ut mul
ta oppida sic præter patarã nõ illustria.Illã nobilé facit de
lubrũ Apollinis quondã opibus & oraculi fide delphico si
mile.Vltra est xanthus flumé & xanthos oppidũ:mós cra
gus:& quæ lyciã finit urbs telmisos.Caria seqt habitat i
certæ originis.Alii idigenas:sunt q pelasgos:qdã cretã exi
stimant:genus usq eo quondã armorũ pugnæq amãs:ut
aliena ét bella mercede ageret:hic castella aliquot sũt.De
inde ,pmótoria duo pedalion & Crya & secũdũ calbin am
nem caunus oppidũ ualitudine habitantiũ isame.Inde ad
alicarnasson hæc adiacét rhodiorum aliquot coloniæ por

the view from it being commanded by Aspendus, a city built by the Argives, and occupied by those living in this area. Here also are the two major rivers, the Oestros and the Cateractes; the Oestros easily navigable, but the other named after its great falls. Between the two lies the city of Perga, containing the temple of Diana, and called by the natives Pergeam. Beyond this is Mount Sardemisos, being close by the town of Phaselis, which was built by Mopsus, and forms the limit of Pamphilia. In sequence is Lycia, named for Lycus, the son of Pandionis. He, in anger, during past times, caused by the fires of the Chymera, had a great bay enclosed from the port town of Sida to the promontory of Taurus. Taurus itself, rises hugely at the shoreline. Thence it carries on the right side toward the north, and on the left toward the south - left and right sides both holding continuously to the west. It joins together many nations within the terminus of its compass, forming their limits where it borders on the sealine. All of these are classed under that name, and also those lands to the east. Thereafter is found Hamodes, Caucasus and Paropamisus. Then is seen the narrows beside the Caspian Sea. Following is Niphates and the Armenian Narrows, and here our own sea again contacts Taurus. Behind this promontory is the river Lymira, and the city of the same name, as well as a number of other towns, little to be regarded, except for Parata. This, in particular, was made noble by the shrine of Apollo, which, on account of its wealth and its oracles, resembles the Delphic Oracle in its fidelity. Thence is the river, Xanthus, with the city Xanthus, and Mount Cragus with the town, Telmisos, forming the border of Lycia. The inhabitants of Caria, which is adjacent, are of unknown origin. To some they are indigenous, to some they are Pelasgian, to others they are Cretan. These Cretans ever fond of arms and war, often served as mercenaries in alien forces. A number of villages follow, and the two promontories, Pedalion and Cyra, by the river, Calbin. Here is the town, Caunus, named for the valor of its inhabitants. Then is Halicarnassus, adjacent to some colonies of the Rhodians.

tus duo gelos:& cui ex urbe:quã amplectit thiſſamiſſa co
gnomen eſt.Inter eos oppidũ larumna & pandion collis
in mare emiſſus:tum tres ex ordine ſinus Tymnias.Sche
nus.Bubeſſus.Tymniæ pmontorium Aphrodiſium eſt.
Schenus ambit hylam.Bubeſſus cynotũ.Gnidus in cornu
pene iſulæ.Interq; eã & ceranicum ſinu i receſſu poſita eu
thenæ.Alicarnaſſos argiuorũ colonia ẽ & cur memorãda
ſit præter conditores:mauſoleum efficit regis mauſoli mo
n umentũ unũ de miraculis ſeptem artemiſiæ opus.Trans
alicarnaſſon illa ſunt littus leuca.urbes mindus. Aryandæ
Neapolis ſinus iaſius & baſilicus.In iaſo ẽ Bargylos. Poſt
baſilicũ ionia aliquot ſe ambagibus ſinuat & primũ a poſ
ſideo pmontorio iſlexũ ichoans cingit oraculũ Apollinis
dictũ olim Branchidæ nunc didymi.Miletũ urbé quondã
ioniæ totius belli paciſq; artibus principé patriã Thaletis
aſtrologi & Timothei muſici & Anaximandri phiſici alio
rũq; ciuium iclytis igeniis merito iclytã:utcũq; Ioniam uo
cant urbé. hyppin amnis mæandri exitũ. Latinũ motem
endymionis a luna:ut ſerũt:adamati fabula nobilé.Dcide
rurſus iſlexa cigit urbé priené & geſi fluminis oſtiũ:moxq;
ut maiore circuitu:ita plura cõplectit.Ibi eſt Panioniũ ſa
cra regio:& ob id eo nomine appellata:q̃ eam cõmuniter
Iones colunt ibi a fugitiuis:ut aiũt cõdita:nomé famæ an
nuit phygela.Ibi epheſus & dianæ clariſſimum templum:
quod Amazones aſia potitæ conſecraſſe tradunt:Ibi cay
ſtros amnis.Ibi lebedos:clariq; Apollinis fanũ:quod mã
to tireſiæ filia fugiens uictores thebanorum. Epigonos &

There are two bays, one known as Gelos and the other as Thissamissa, each haven being named for the town nearest. Placed between is the city of Larumna by the hill Pandion, which projects toward the sea. Then come three bays in order: Thymnias, Schenus and Bubessus. At the promontory of Tymniae is Aphrodisium. Scheus, then, borders the ambit of Hylam, Bubessus and Cynotus. Gnidus stands at the tip of the peninsula. Within the bay is Ceranicum, nearly enclosed, and it lies near to Euthena. Halicarnassus is colonized by the Argives, and why it is to be memorialized has to do with its founders and with the construction of the Mausoleum. It is the tomb of King Mausoleus, built by Queen Artemisia, and it stands as one of the seven wonders of the world. Past Halicarnassus, and along the sea line, is Leuca, and the cities of Mindus, Aryanda and Naples, with the bays of Iasius and Basilicus. In Iasius is found the town of Bargylos. After Basilicus, the ambit of Ionia follows a winding course, beginning at the promontory of Possideus, it turns to encompass the area of the Oracle of Apollo. In previous times this was known as Branchida, but is now called Didymus. The city of Miletus - at one time the leader of all Ionia whether in the arts of war or peace - was the fatherland of Thales the astrologer, Timothy the musician and Anaximander the philosopher. Other minds of great merit were also native to that city called Ionia. The town Hyppin is by the river Meander at its entry into the sea. Mount Latmus, situated at that point, is famed for the tale of Endymion, beloved by the Moon. The fable is adamantly held. From there, the course of the bay encircles the city Priene by the mouth of the river Gesi. Widening into a larger circuit, it then encompasses the sacred land of Panionius, a name accepted in common by all the inhabitants in Ionia. Thence is a city supposed to have been founded by fugitives, and called, by general assent, Phygela. Here stands Ephesus, and the most famed of all temples to Diana. The Amazons, when they ruled Asia, consecrated it by the river, Caystros. Here is Lebedos, and the temple of Apollo Clarius. It was built by Manto, the daughter of Tiresis, in a flight from the Epigoni after the Theban victory.

colophon quã.Mopſus eiuſdẽ mãtos filius ſtatuit:ad p̃/
montoriũ:quo finus claudit̃:qd̃ altera pte aliũ: quẽ ſmyr
næum uocãt:efficit:anguſtiſq̨ ceruicibus reliqua extendit
in latius abit in peninſulæ faciẽ ſup anguſtias hinc ceos il/
linc clazomena.& qa terga agunt cõfinio adnexa mari di
uerſis frontibus diuerſa maria p̃ſpectat.In ipſa peninſula
eſt Coryna.in finu ſmyrnæo ẽ thermodon amnis: & urbs
Leuca.extra phocis ioniæ ultima: Proxia regio ex quo ab
æolis incoli cœpit æolis facta:ante myſia:& qua hellespõ/
tum attigit troianis poſſidnetibus troas fuit.Primã urbẽ a
myrino conditore myrinã uocãt. Sequentẽ Pelops ſtatuit
uicto œnomao reuerſus ex græcia. Cymen noiauit pulſis
q habitarant:dux amazonũ cyme. ſupra caicus iter eleam
decurrit & pytanẽ illã:quæ archeſilã tulit nihil affirmantis
achademiæ clariſſimũ antiſtitẽ. Tũ in pmontorio ẽ Can/
na oppidũ:quod præteruectos ſinus excipit non paruus:
ſed longe ac molliter flexus retrahẽſq̨ paulatim oras uſq̨
ad ima montis idæ:Iſthmos paruis urbibus aſpſus eſt:qua
rũ clariſſima eſt ciſtena gremio iteriore campus thebe no
mine adrymetion auſtrã.ereſſam oppida eodẽ:quo dicta
ſunt ordine:adiacẽtia continet.In altero latere Antandrũ
duplex cauſa nominis iactat̃.alii Aſcaniũ Aeneæ filiũ: cũ
ibi regnaret:captũ a pelaſgis ea ſe redemiſſe cõmemorãt.
Alii ab iis putant conditã:quos ex Andro inſula uis & ſe
ditio excegerat.Hi antãdrũ quaſi p andro.Illi quaſi p uiro
accipi uolunt. Sequẽs tractus tãgit gargara & aſſon ætolo/
rũ colonias.Tũ ſinus alter alchæo limẽ ñ lõge ab ilio litto

Regarding the city of Colophon (this Mopsus was, himself, the son of Manto) he caused another such structure to be built on the promontory by the narrows of the harbor at the place known as Smyrna. From here, the projecting forelands jut out sharply, and then widen toward Ceus and thence to Clazomene. The reverse side of the bayshore lies in a confinement by the sealine, and runs along with diverse fronts toward the ocean. In the peninsula itself is Coryna, and within the bay of Smyrna is the river Thermodon with the city Leca. Past this is Phocis which forms the terminus of Ionia. In proximity to this region is the land first colonized by the Aeolians, and called now Aeolis; but in times past was called Mysia. At the place where it touches the Hellespont, the locale was once held by the Trojans, and is known, therefore, as Troas. Its first city is called Myrina, identified by the name of its founder, Myrinus. Subsequently, Pelops built it; this was following his return from Greece, and his victory there over the king, Oenomaus. Cyme was so named when its former inhabitants had been driven out by Cyme, the leader of the Amazons. Beyond here flows the stream, Caicus, coursing between Elean and Pytane, and it was here that Archesilaus was born. He was that renowned high priest of the Academy who taught that nothing could be affirmed with certainty. Then, at the promontory, is the city of Canna. In passing this point, the bay widens in no small measure, but at great length it forms a curve of various inlets, and advanced toward the land even to the base of Mount Ida. The isthmus contains a scattering of small towns, among them Cistena is to be noted. At its interior is found the field known as Thebes, and along this tract are the towns, Adrymetium, Austra and Erassam, lying adjacent in that order. To the other side is Antandrus. Two reasons are given for this name. Some say that Canius, son of Aeneas, named it during his rule for his rescue from the Pelasgians. Others say the builders came from Andros, from which they were expelled for sedition. The name, then, should be Andros, not the name of the man. Then comes the tract by Gargara and Assos, held by Aetolians. Opposite is Alcheus, near Ilion,

ra icuruat urbe bello excidioᛩ clariſſima. Hic Sygeū fuit
oppidū. hic achiuorū fuit bellātiū ſtatio. Huc ab ideo mō
te demiſſus Scamander exit & Simois fama q̄ natura ma
iora flumina. Ipſe mons uetere diuarū certamie & iudicio
paridis memoratus orientē ſolē aliter:q̄ ĩ aliis terris ſolet
aſpici oſtētat. nāᛩ ex ſūmo uertice eius ſpeculantibus pe
ne a media nocte ſparſi ignes paſſim micare:& ut lux ap
propinquat. ita coirc ac ſe cōiungcre uidentˀ:donec magis
magi ſᛩ collecti pauciores ſubide & una ad poſtremū flā
ma ardeāt. ea cū diu clara & icēdio ſimilis effulſit:cogit ſe
ac rotundat: & fit igens globus. diuis quoᛩ grandis & ter
ris adnexus apparet:deide paulatĩ decreſcēs & quāto decre
ſcit:eo clarior fugat nouiſſie noctem:& cū die iā ſol factus
attollit . Extra ſinū ſunt rhetæa littora a Rhetæo & darda
nia claris urbibus. Aiacis tamen ſepulchro maxie illuſtria.
Ab his ſit arctius mare:nec iam abluit terras:ſed rurſus di
uidens anguſto hclleſpōti freto littus obuiū findit:facitᛩ
ut iterū terræ:qua fluit:latera ſint. Inter ius bithyni ſunt &
mariādynei. In ora graiæ urbes abydos & lāpſacum & pa
rion & priapos. Abidos magni quōdā amoris cōmertio i
ſignis ē. Lāpſacū phocœis appellātibus nomē ex eo traxit
q̓ cōſulentibus i quaſnā terras potiſſimū tēderēt. res ſpon
ſum erat ubi primū fulſiſſet:ibi ſedē capeſcere. Tum rurſus
fit apertius mare propontis. In id Granicus effunditur pu
gna:quæ primum inter perſas & Alexandrum fuit: nobi
lis. Trans amnem ſedet in ceruice peninſulæ cyzicum no
men cyzicus indidit:quem a minyis imprudentibus: cum

and, on this shore, the war and sack of the great city (Troy) had taken place. Here is the city of Sigeum, the place where the Achaeans were stationed during the war. Here, too, the river, Scamander flows down from Mount Ida, with its tributary, the Simois - major streams in this country. Of itself, the Mount, long ago, had been the scene of contention among the goddesses, and it was due to the judgment of Paris that, among other things, this memorial to the eastern sun should also be seen in other lands. Indeed, from the summit of its height it would appear to observers, during the middle of the night, as the vision of many scattered fires glittering everywhere. With the approach of daylight, they are seen to draw together in union, and, finally, collect into one. This, however, subsides, and it faintly dissolves into a shining. The refulgent illumination burns, flaming and rotund, until it forms a planet. For a time it seems grand and huge, joined as one to the world. But, by small degrees, the sun appears more clear and bright, and, at last, it drives away the night. Past the bay is the coastline of the Rhetaens, with their famed cities, Rhetaeus and Dardania. Here is the sepulchre of their most illustrious Ajax. At this point the sea is constricted, not washing in at the land, but reversing, it divides itself at the strait of the Hellespont. With that, it flows into bodies of water on each side. To the interior is Bithynia and the Mariadynes. At the coastline are the Greek cities, Abydos, Lampsacus, Parion and Priapos. Abydos was known for its commerce in love (Hero and Leander), and the Phoceans gave this name to Lampsacus. Advice was asked with regard to the land they might best travel to. The response was made that they should dwell wherever lightning might first strike. Widening again, the sea opens at the Propontis. Here the river, Granicus flows, and here was the first battle fought between the Persians and Alexander. Across the stream lies the neck of the peninsula, Cyzicus, named after Cyzicus. It was through the imprudence of the Minyans, when they were

colchos peterēt fufum acie cæfūcʒ accepimus. Poſt placia
& Scylace paruæ pelafgorū coloniæ:qbus a tergo iminet
mons olympus ut icolæ uocant.Myſius flumen rhynda cū
in quæ ſequuntur emittit. Circa angues naſcunt imanes
necʒ ob magnitudinē modo:ſed ob id ēt mira biles:cʒ ubi
in alueū eius æſtus ſolécʒ fugerunt emergūt atcʒ hiant ſu
peruolantefcʒ aues:quáuis alte & perniciter ferant abſor
bēt.Trans rhyndacum eſt Dafcylos &quā colophonii col
locauere myrlea.Duo ſunt ide modiciſinus:alter ſine no
mine cion amplectitur Phrygiæ haud longe iacentis op
portuniſſimum empo riū:alter olbianos in promontorio
fert Neptūni fanū:in gremio aſtacon a megarēſibus con
ditam.Deinde priores terræ iterū iacent exituricʒ in pon
tum pelagi canalis anguſtior.Europā ab Aſia ſtadiis qᷠncʒ
diſterminat thracius:ut dictum eſt bofphorus. Ipſis i fau
cibus oppidum in ore templum eſt:Oppidi nomen chal
cedon.auctor Archias megarenſium princeps:templi nu
men Iuppiter conditore Iaſone. Hic iā ſeſe igens pontus
aperit:niſi qua promontoria ſunt:huc atcʒ illuc longo re
ctocʒ limite extentus ſinuatus cætera.Sed qa contra mi
nus quā ad læuā & dextra abſceſſit mollibufcʒ faſtigiis do
nec anguſtos utrincʒ angulos faciat iflectitur:ad formam
ſcytici arcus maxime incuruus.breuis.atrox.nebuloſus ra
ris ſtationibus:non molli neque arenoſo circundatus lit
tore:uicinus aquilonibus:& quia non profundus eſt. flu
ctuoſus atque feruens:olim excolentium ſæuo admodum
igenio axenus:poſt cōmertio aliarum gentiū mollitis ali

bound for Colchis, that they had slain the man there. This, at least, is our understanding of the matter. Beyond here is Placia and Scylace, small colonies of the Pelasgians. Standing at the back of them looms Mount Olympus, so it is called by the populace. The Mysius, along with the river Rhyndacus, water those lands lying to the front. Native to this area are immense serpents, not only remarkable in size, but also striking in behaviour. To the river channel they will flee to escape the summer heat, and there, with jaws gaping open, prey upon those birds swiftly flying over. By the Rhyndacus is Dascylus, a city built by the Colophonians, along with their town, Myrlea. Two bays are found here, the one is without a name, surrounding the city, Cion. The other, larger, lies by the merchant town of Phrygia, which is not a great distance from Olbianos. At the promontory is the temple of Neptune; sited within the bay is the town Astacon, which the Megarians had founded. Thence, the land widens again, and forms a narrow flow, open to the sea at Pontus. Europe and Asia stand divided by the length of only five stadia here at this point in Thrace, usually called the Bosphorus. Built on the shore of the isthmus is a temple, and the city is Chalcedon. Its founder was Archius, the prince of the Megarians. The statue in the temple is that of Jupiter, and its sculptor was Jason. At this locale the sea spreads itself wide - except at the promontories, and extends far on either side, sweeping along the shore, but gradually arcs in a return. To no great extent does it carry straight, but, in a turning manner, draws into a strait again so as to resemble a Scythian bow. Few harbors are seen along this sparse coastline. No soft sandy shore here, but only the north country - atrocious, fogbound and forlorn. Since the water does not run deep, the surf is always wild. In times of old, because of the nature of the land and its dwellers, it was called Axenus (Inhospitable). Yet later, through commerce with other peoples, some degree of mollification

Liber Primus.

quintum moribus dictus euximus. In eo primum marian/
dynei urbem habitant ab argiuo:ut ferunt: Hercule datã
heraclæa uocitatur:id famæ quidem adiecit.Iuxta specus ē
achærusia ad manos:ut aiunt:peruius:atq; inde extractum
Cerberū existimant.Tum tios oppidum milesiorū quidē
colonia:sed iam soli gentisq; paphlagonū:quorū in litto/
ribus pene mediis promontorium est Carambis:citra Par
thenius amnis. urbes sesamus & Cromna:& acithisoro/
phryxi filio posita cythoros.Tum cimolis accolit. & quæ
paphlagoniam finit armenæ. Chalybes proximi clarissi/
mas habent amyson:& synopen cynici Diogenis patriam
amnes alyn & thermodonta.Secundum alyn urbs est ly/
casto.a thermodonte campus. In eo fuit themisyrum op/
pidum.fuere & Amazonum castra ideo amazonū uocant
Tabereni calybas attigunt:quibus in risu lusuque summū
bonum est.Vltra carambin Mossynœci turres ligneas su/
beunt.notis corpus omne persignant.propatulo uescun/
tur.promiscue concumbunt.& palam reges suffragio deli
gunt:uinculisque & arctissima custodia tenent. Atque ubi
culpam praue imperando meruere:inedia diei totius affi/
ciunt:Cæterum asperi.inculti. pernoxii appulsis. Deinde
minus feri uerum & hi inconditis moribus Macrocepha
li.Discheri.Buxedi.Rare urbes Cerasus & Trapezus ma/
xime illustres. Inde his locus est ubi finem ductus a bos/
phoro tractus accipit: atque inde se in sinu aduersi litto/
ris flexus attollens angustissimum ponti facit angulum.
Hic sunt colchi:hinc phasis erumpit:hic eodem nomine

did take place in their manners, and so thereafter it came to be called Euxinus (Hospitable).
Here, in the first place, is the city which the Miriandynes occupy, given to them by
Hercules of Argos, and thus called Heraclea. This account is widely credited. In close
proximity is the cavern of Acherusia, which is reported to lead to the underworld.
Cerberus is said to have been extracted from it. Then is the city of Tios, once colonized
by the Milesians, but now held solely by the Paphlagonians. They have the seacoast
almost to the promontory, Carambis. Nearby is the river, Parthenius, with the cities,
Sesamus, Cromna and Cytorus; this last was built by Cithisorus who was the son of
Phrixus. Then, following, is Cimolis, which forms the boundary of Paphlagonia at
Armenia. The tribe of the Chalybes, living in proximity, possess two noteworthy cities,
Amyson and Synope. Diogenes, the cynic, was born in this area. Here, also, are the
rivers Halys and Thermodon. Following Halys is the town of Lycasto. But adjacent to
Thermodon is the open plain on which was once the city of Themiscyra. Here the
Amazons encamped, and hence it is called Amazonia. Bordering along by the Chalybes
are the Tabernians, whose chief accomplishment would seem to be in games and
amusement. Past the promontory of Carambis dwell the Mossynecians, living in wooden
turrets. They decorate their bodies with all manner of markings; they consume their food
out of doors, and exist in promiscuous cohabitation. They elect their kings by open
suffrage, after which, he is kept in close custody. When he is guilty of misconduct, he is
then compelled to fast an entire day for his offence. For the others, they reject everyone -
uncivilized themselves - and spurn everyone approaching. Beyond them are tribes less
wild, but still uncivilized: Macrocephalans, Discherians and Buxedians. Few cities are
here: Cerasus and Trapezus. From here the coast draws away from the Bosphorus, and
advances forward, only to reverse into a broad inlet. Then, forming another strait, it flows
to Pontus. Here are the Colchians, near the river, Phasis. Here, too, and bearing the same
name

quo atmnis est athenistagora milesio deductu oppidu: hic
phryxi templu & lucus fabula uetere pellis aureæ nobilis.
Hinc orti montes longo se iugo & donec ripheis coniun
gant : exporrigunt: q altera parte i Euxinu & mæotida &
tanaï. Altera in caspiu pelagus obuersi cerauni dicunt iidé
aliubi. Taurici. Moschi. amazoici. caspii. Caraxici. caucasi:
ut aliis aliisue appositis gentibus ita aliis aliisq; dicti nomi
nibus. At i prio flexu ia curui littoris oppidu est:qd graeci
mercatores constituisse: & qa cu cæca tepestate agerentur:
ignaris: quæ terra esset: cygni uox notá dederat: cygnu ap/
pellasse dicunt. Reliqua eius feræ icultæq; gentes uasto ma
re assidentes tenent. Melachlæni terrestrea. sex solitæ: co
raxi. Pthirophagi. hæniochi. achæi. cercetici:et i consinio
meotidis syndoes. In hæniochoru finibus dioscorias a Ca
store & Polluce pontu cu Iasone igressis. Syndos i syndo/
nu ab ipsis terraru cultoribus condita est:obliqua tunc re/
gio & i latu modice patens iter pontu paludéq; ad bospho
rum excurrit:quá duobus alueis i lacu & i mare psluès co/
rocondamá pene insulá reddit. Q uattuor urbes ibi sunt
hermonassa. Cepo ephanagoria: & i ipso ore cimeriu. hac
ingressos lacus accipit lóge lateq; diffusus. Q ua terras tan
git icuruo circudatus littore:qua mari propior est: nisi ubi
apit : quasi margine obductus citra magitudiné ppe poto
similis. Orá quæ a bosphoro ad tanain usq; deflectit mæo
tici icolut toreatæ. arichi. phicores & ostio fluminis pximi
Iaxamatæ. apud eos easdé arte fœmiæ:qs uiri exercét adeo
ut ne militia qdé uacét. Viri pedib9 ihærét: sagittisq; depu

as that of the river (Phasis), is a city built by Athenistagoras of Miletus. It is the site of the temple of Phryxus, and a sacred grove which is connected with the ancient fable of the golden fleece. From this place rises a long ridge of mountains until they join with the Ryphanian range. These extend, on the one extreme, from around the Euxinus, Maeotis and Tanais, and then terminate, on the other extreme, at the Caspian. They are called the Cerauni. Yet other names also exist for them: Taurici, Moschi, Amazoni, Caspiani, Caraxici or Caucasian - the name depending on whose area the peaks are passing through. But at the first turn in its bending course is a city which Greek merchants once built. They were cast ashore here when their light vessel was driven aground during a tempest, and they did not know what land they were in. Directly, they heard the voice of a swan, and therefore called the place Cygnus. The remaining nations living beyond this vast sea are wild and savage, and are termed the Melanthians. Farther from them are the brutal and solitary Coraxi, the Pithirophagi, the Haniochi, the Achaei, and the Cercetici. Within the confines of the Maeotis live the Syndones. Within the confines of the Haeniochori is the city of Dioscurias, which was founded by Castor and Pollux when they entered into this sea with Jason. The city of Syndos, standing at the borderland of the Syndones nation, was built by the peoples of that place. Then, at an oblique to this region, and spreading laterally, is that tract which appears between the Pontine Marshes and the Bosphorus. These two form the basin between the river and the sea, and, between them, very nearly make Corocondama an island. There are four cities here: Hermonassa, Cepo, Ephanagoria and, at the inlet, Cimmerium. Travellers here find a lake, wide and long, then, curving finally to the sea, and it would seem to undercut its own bankside. Its size is similar, if smaller, than Pontus. At the coast from Bosphorus to Tanais, by the curvature, is Maeotis; this is held by the Toreates, the Arichi, the Phicores and, at the outlet, the Iaxamathians. Among these last named, the women perform just as the men in the military. The men fight on foot with arrows.

gant. Illæ equeftre prælium ineunt:nec ferro dimicant:fed
quos laqueis intercepere:trahendo conficiunt. Nubunt. ta
men. Verum ut nubiles habeant :non i ætate modus eft:
nifi quæ hofte iteremere:uirgines manet. Ipfe Tanais ex
rhipheo monte deiectus adeo præceps ruit:ut cum uicina
flumina cum mæotis & bofphorus:tum ponti aliqua bru⸗
mali rigore durentur:folus æftus hyeméq; iuxta ferens idé
femper & fublimis incitatufque decurrat. Ripas eius fauro
matæ & ripis hærentia poffident. Vna gens:aliquot popu
li & aliquot nomina. Primi mæotici. Gynæcocratumenoe
Regna amazonum fœcundos pabulo. At alia fteriles nu⸗
dofq; campos tenent budini. Geloni urbem ligneam ha⸗
bitant. Iuxta thiffagetæ turceq; uaftas filuas occupant:alun
turq; uenando. Tum continuis rupibus late afpera : & de⸗
ferta regio ad arempheos ufq; permittitur. His iuftiffimi
mores. Pro domibus nemora. Aliméta baccæ:& maribus
& fœminis nuda funt capita. Sacri itaq; habentur: adeoq;
ipfos nemo de tam feris gentibus uiolat:ut aliis quoq; ad
eos confugiffe pro afylo fit. Vltra furgit mons rhipheus:
ultraq; eum iacet ora:quæ fpectat oceanum.

Pomponii Melæ de fitu orbis. Liber Secundus.

SIAE In noftrum mare Tanainq; uergentis
quem dixi finis ac fitus é:ac per eundem am
nem in mæotida remeantibus ad dextram
Europæ modo finiftro latere in nauigantiũ
appofita ac rhipheis montibus proxima:&

The women enter the battlefield on horseback - not to contend with swords, but to intercept with netting, and to draw the enemy down with reins. They marry at the nubile stage, not by assent among their peers, instead, only after they have slain an enemy. Until such time they remain virgins. That river, the Tanais, racing down in its mighty rush from Mount Rhipheus, cascades headlong throughout the season when the winter ice has frozen solid all other rivers in the country: the Maeotis, the Bosphorus and parts of Pontus. It alone, summer and winter, bears forward at full surge in its high swell. Its banks, and those countries inherent along its banks, are referred to as the Sauromatians. These are various types and various peoples, with differing names. First come the Maeotici, those who deal in women, and here is found the realm of the Amazons, with fertile pasture lands. Otherwise, the more sterile and unproductive fields are held by the Budini. The Geloni inhabit their city of wood. Next are the Thissageti, who, along with the Turks, occupy a vast forestland, where they live as hunters. Then, continuing along the widespread riverbank, are the Aremphei, living in a waste region. Their manners are uncommon. Instead of houses they dwell in groves, and live on berries; men and women alike go about with heads uncovered. Nonetheless, they are held to be holy, and no one from those wild lands may dare harm them, lest the others fly to them as though for asylum. Beyond here rises Mount Rhipheus, and, beyond it, lies the coast line overlooking the ocean.

THE SECOND BOOK

Pomponius Mela: The Situation of the World

Asia, at the River Tanais, verges upon our own sea, as I have stated previously. This stream, joining back to the Maeotis, has Europe directly to its right hand, and, to its left hand, the entirely navigable waterway positioned in close proximity to Mount Rhipheus,

huc enim pertinent. Cadętes affiduo niues adeo in uia ef/
ficiunt: ut ultra ne uifum quidę itendentium admittant.
Deíde eft regio ditis admodũ foli inhabitabilis tamen:qa
gryphi fæuũ & pertinax ferarũ genus aurum terra penitus
egeſtũ mire amant mireq; cuſtodiunt:& funt infeſti attin
gentibus. Hominũ primi funt Scytæ: fcytharumque quis
finguli oculi cę dicuntur arimafpę. Ab eis Effedones ufq;
ad mæotida. Huius flexũ huges amnis fecat. Agathyrfi &
fauromatæ ambiunt:quia pro fedibus plauſtra habent di/
ćti hamaxobitæ:obliqua tunc ad bofphorum plaga excur
rens ponto ac mæotide includitur. In paludę uergentia fa
tharchæ tenent. In bofphorum cimerica oppida myrmeti
on:panticapeum theodofia: hermifium. In euxinũ mare
taurici:fuper eos finus portuofus & ideo calos limen ap/
pellatus promontoriis duobus includitur:alterum criu me
topon uocant:Carambico:quod i Afia diximus:patet ad/
uerfum. Parthenion alterũ oppidũ adiacet Cheronefus a
Diana:fi credatur:conditũ. & nympheo fpecu:q; in ærce
eius Nymphis facratũ eſt: maxime illuſtre. Subit tũ ripam
mare & donec quinque milia paffuũ abfit a mæotide refu
gientia ufque fubfequens littora:qua fatarchæ & taurici te
nent:peninfulam reddit. Q uod inter paludem & finũ ę.
Taphræ nominatur. Sinus carcinites:in eo urbs eſt carci/
ne: quam duo flumina Gerros & Hypacyris uno oſtio
effluentia attingunt: uerum diuerfis fontibus & aliunde
delapfi. Nam gerros inter bafilidas & nomadas euoluitur
Siluæ deinde funt:quas maximas hæ terræ ferunt:& pan/

which extends, indeed, to this point. Falling without cease, the snows not only make for heavy going, but also make difficult any depth of vision by those approaching. Beyond this is a region quite rich in fertility, yet with only one sort of inhabitants. Here live the Gryphi - little more than savage beasts - but they own deposits of gold, which they greatly love, and these are to be found lying within the ground. Punishment is inflicted on any of those nations which might touch it. Primarily, these men are classed as Scythian, but among these Scythians are those who are said to possess only a single eye, the Arimaspians. From their sector, the Essedonians hold to the Maeotis. The river, Huges intersects here at a particular bend. In this tract occupy the Agathyrsi and the Sauromatians, who, because they travel about seated in wagons, are called the Hamaxobitians. Then, at an oblique, the region runs toward the Bosphorus, and touches both Pontus and Maeotis. Near the verge of this swampland live the Satarchae. By the Cimmerian Bosphorus are the cities of Myrmetion, Panticapeum, Theodosia and Hermisium. At the Euxine Sea are the Taurians, and past them is a bay with two promontories, therefore called the blessed lake. Two promontories are found here - the one is Criumetopon, close to Carambis, which, as I have stated, is in Asia, and the other is Cheronesus, which is near to the promontory, Parthenion. The city was built by Diana, if this account should be credited. At the summit is the cavern Nymphaeum, held sacred to the Nymphs, and widely renowned. The sea then undercuts the river bank to a length of five miles, and subsequently reversing, bears toward Maeotis. It passes the holdings of both the Satarchians and the Taurians, and returns, with that, to the peninsula. Between the swamp and the bay is the area of Taphrae, and the bay is known as Carcinites. Here is a city of the same name, at which, are seen two rivers, the Gerros and the Hypacyris. These join, and flow as one harbor, having previously come from separate headwaters. The Gerros evolves between the Basilides and the Nomads. Forests are in this sector, and they stand through much of the country.

ticapes: qui nomadas georgofque difterminat.Terra tum
longe diftenta excedens tenui radice littori adnectit .Poft
fpaciofa modice paulatim feipfa faftigiat: & quafi in mu
cronem longa colligens latera facie pofiti enfis allecta eft.
Achilles infefta claffe mare ponticum ingreffus ibi ludi
cro cettamine celebraffe uictoriam:& cum ab armis quies
erat:fe ac fuos curfu exercitauiffe memoratur:ideo dicta e
dromos achilleos. Tum boryfthenes gentem fui nomi
nis abluit iter fcythiae amnes amœniffimus: turbidis aliis
liquidiffimus defluit.Placidior quã cæteri potarique pul
cherrimus.Alit lætiffima pabula magnofque pifces: qui
bus & optimus fapor:& nulla offa funt.Longe uenit igno
tifque ortus e fontibus quadraginta dierũ iter alueo ftrin
git:tantoque fpatio nauigabilis fecundum Boryftenida &
Olbida græca oppida egreditur.Calipidas hypanis inclu
dit.Ex grandi palude oritur:quã matrem eius accolæ ap
pellant:& diu qualis natus eft:defluit.Tantũ non longe a
mari ex paruo fonte:cui exampheo cognomen eft. Adeo
amaras aquas accipit:ut ipfe quoque iã fui diffimilis & nõ
dulcis hinc defluat.Axiaces proximus intra calipidas axia
cafque defcendit.Hos ab iftricis Tyra feparat:furgit i Neu
ris:qua exit:fui nominis oppidum attingit.At ille:quis cy
thiæ populos a fequentibus dirimit apertis in Germania:
fontibus alio:quã definit:nomine exoritur.Nam per ima
nia magnarum gentiũ diu danubius eft. Deinde aliter ap
pellatibus accolis Ifter fit: acceptifque aliquot amnibus in
gens iam & eorum:qui in noftrũ mare decidunt: tantum

The Panticapes, a river, separates the Nomads from the Georgians. The country then spreads far and wide, but, at length, closes into a land spit at the sea shore. Thereupon, opening to an extent, it advances to somewhat resemble a gable, and appears as a sword laid flat on its side. Achilles, with an incursion by means of a sea-borne force, entered the Pontine Sea here, and caused this victory to be celebrated by games. He, along with his men, ran in races as a fit memorial; wherefore it has come to be called the Track of Achilles. Then, the river Borysthenius flows through a nation of the same name, and, among the Scythian waterways, this is the most pleasant. Whereas the others are turgid and swollen, this runs placid and clear to drink. It is rich in pasturelands and plentiful in fish; these fish are delicious and free of bones. In its length, it rises from some unknown spring. Forty days are needed to traverse its navigable stream, as far as to the city of Borysthenius, and to the Greek town, Olbida at the bay. The river Calipidas is included in the stream which issues from the bog Hypanis. Out of this great swamp rises that deluge which the people, living in the area, refer to as its mother. Indeed, the two seem to flow at length as they were born so. At some distance, not far from the sea, is the small spring called Exampheus. From it, bitter waters are produced, and this tributary renders the main course downstream undrinkable. The Axiaces tribe is next, found between the Calipidas waterway and the river Axiaces. These are then separated by the stream Tyra from the Istricanians, and the stream has its headwaters among the tribes of the Neuri. Where it makes its exit, a town is found bearing the same name. The water system, itself, which divides the Scythian peoples from all other tribes following after in sequence, has its primal spring located in Germania. Originating through the range of the Imans it is known to the large nations there as the Danube. Thereafter, it is variously named as the various tribes may choose; being known as the river Ister at the place where it enters. Yet is accepts, in turn, many water courses. At last, it descends into our own sea as the greatest

Nilo minor totidé:quot ille oſtiis:ſed tribus tenuibus:re⁄
liqs nauigabilibus effluit.Ingenia cultuſq; gétiũ differunt.
Eſſedones funera parentũ læti & uictimis ac feſto coitu fa
miliarium celebrant.Corpora ipſa laniata & cæſis pecorũ
uiſceribus imixta epulando coñſumunt. Capita ubi fabre
expoliuere auro iuncta pro poculis gerunt.Hæc ſunt apud
eos ipſos pietatis ultima officia.Agathyrſi ora artuſq; pin
gunt:ut quique maioribus præſtant:ita magis uel minus.
Cæterũ iiſdé omnes notis:& ſic ut ablui nequeant. Sarma
tæ auri argentiq; maximarũ peſtium ignari uice rerũ com⁄
mertia exercent.atque obſæua hyemis admodũ aſſidue de
merſis in humum ſedibus ſpecus aut ſuffoſſa habitant. To
tum brachati corpus:& niſi qua uident etiam ora ueſtiti.
Tauri Iphigeniæ & Oreſtis aduentu maxime memorati
immanes ſunt moribus: immanemq; famam habent. So
lere pro uictimis aduenas cædere.Baſilidiis ab Hercule:&
echidna generis principia ſunt:Mores regii.Arma tantum
ſagittæ.Vagi nomades pecorũ pabula ſequuntur:atque ut
illa pecorũ durant:ita diu ſtatã ſedé agunt.Colunt georgi
exercentq; agros.Axiace furari qd ſit ignorant.Ideoq; nec
ſua cuſtodiunt.nec aliena contingunt.Interius habitantiũ
ritus aſperior & incultior regio eſt.Bella cædeſque amant.
Moſq; eſt bellantibus cruoré eius:quem primũ intereme⁄
runt ipſis e uulneribus ebibere:ut quiſque plures intereme
rit:ita apud eos habetur eximius. Cæterũ ex parté eſſe cæ⁄
dis inter opprobria uel maximũ:ne fœdera qdé incruenta
ſunt.ſauciant ſe:q paciſcunt :exéptũq; ſanguiné:ubi pmi⁄

of them all - minor to none but the Nile. Its delta touches the sea by three mouths, some of them navigable. The indigenous population here all differ by culture. The Essedones, at the funeral of their parents, happily make offerings, and, with feasting among their families, they celebrate. The corpses are then butchered, and intermixed with the intestines of flock animals, and consumed as though at a banquet. But their heads are fashioned into adornment, bound about with gold, in order to serve as drinking vessels. This act is considered the ultimate office of their piety. The Agathyrsi paint their mouths and arms in order to show to any superiors an enhanced appearance, to a greater or less extent. They all so decorate, and the markings cannot be washed away. The Sarmatians, not being acquainted with the evils of gold and silver, have commerce with one another by direct exchange. Because of the bitterly cold winters, they have their habitations below the ground or within caves and caverns. All their bodies are covered in great breeches, with just their eyes barely visible. The Taurians - being remembered primarily for the coming of Iphigenia and Orestes - are made famous by their inhuman savagery. Customarily, they slay, as their victims, any strangers coming among them. The Basilides originate, as a tribe, from Hercules and Echidna, and their manners are likewise regal. Their weapons are arrows alone. Vagabond nomads, they follow after their grazing herds, and dwell there so long as the pasture remains. The Georgians, however, practice the cultivation of fields. The Axiaces do not have any understanding of stealing, and therefore, do not have custody of their own goods, nor do they touch another's. Those dwelling upland from them occupy an inferior region, less given to cultivation. They are lovers of warfare and killing. Their custom is to draw blood from those fallen in battle, and to drink from the wounds. They suppose the best among them to be those who have slain the greatest number. The rest, who avoid the slaughter, suffer the greatest opprobrium. The most deeply binding covenants and federations are also solemnized with bloodletting. A pact is sealed by bloody gashes which flow together,

ſcuere deguſtãt. Id putãt manſuræ fidei pignus certiſſimũ.
Inter epulas:quot qſque iter fecerit:referre lætiſſima & fre
quétiſſima mentio:biniſque poculis:q plurimos retulere:
ppotatis iterlocantur honos præcipuus eſt. pocula ut Eſdo
nes parentũ ita inimiciſſimorũ capitibus expoliunt. Apud
anthropophagos ipſæ etiam epulæ uiſceribus humanis ap
parantur. Geloni hoſtium cutibus equos ſeque uelant. Il
los reliqui corporis:ſe capitum. Melanclænis atra ueſtis &
ex ea nomen. Neuris ſtati ſingulis tempus eſt:quo ſi uelint
in lupos:iterũꝗ in eos:qui fuere mutentur. Mars omniũ
deus. Ei pro ſimulacris enſes & tentoria dedicant: homi
neſque pro uictimis feriunt. Terræ late patent & ob exce
dentia ripas ſuas plerũꝗ flumia nuſquã non ad pabula fer
tiles. Alicubi uſque adeo ſteriles ad cætera:ut qui habitant
lignorũ egentes ignes oſſibus alant. His thracia pxima é:
eaꝗ a pontici lateris fronte uſꝗ in illyricos penitus imiſſa
qua latera agit iſtro pelagoꝗ contingitur. Regio nec cœlo
læta nec ſolo:& niſi qua mari propior eſt:infœcunda frigi
da:eorumque:quæ feruntur maligne admodum patiens:
raro uſquã pomiferam arborem:uitem frequentius tole
rat:ſed nec eius quidem fructus maturat ac mitigat:niſi ubi
frigora obicctu frondium cultores arcuere:Viros benigni
us alit nõ ad ſpeciem tamen. Nam & illis aſper atque ide
cens corporum habitus eſt. Cæterum ad ferociam & nume
rum:ut multi imiteſque ſint : maxime ferax. Paucos am
nes:q í pelagus euadũt:uerũ celeberrimos hebrũ & neſton
ſtrymona emittit. Montes íterior attollit hæmon & Rho

commingled. It is supposed - when all this sluice is swallowed down - to certify complete fidelity. With regard to the feasts which they make, it brings them the greatest pleasure and common fellowship to employ two drinking vats, and each man recounts, with embellishment, the tale of his slaughters. Afterward, the vats are consumed. Just as the Essedonians drink from the heads of their parents, so these savages use the skulls of their enemies. Concerning the Anthropophagi, they are ever ready to feast upon human viscera. The Gelonians cover their horses and themselves with the skins of the enemy - their own heads with the scalps, and the animals with the remainder. The Melanchanes vest themselves all in black, and from this, are given the Melancholy name. The Neuri establish one singular time period during which they can choose to become wolves; after this, they can again mutate back into their former selves. Mars is the deity for them all. But to him, rather than any images, they dedicate their swords and tents, and offer human victims. The landmass here spreads open widely, and the river systems often overflow on this floodplain; nowhere does it fail to leave behind a fertile pasture land. Nonetheless, all the rest still remains a sterile barren, and the inhabitants there, who lack wood, must use bones for kindling. The Thracians are in near proximity to them, and their holdings run from the shore of Pontus even to the Illyrians. The tract is closed within itself by the river Ister and by the sea. The region is blessed by neither heaven nor earth. Other than where it touches the seashore, it is infertile and frigid, and suffers from every manner of malignancy. Rare indeed is the fruit tree. But the area does bear vines, however, these do not show mature growth, nor do they propagate. The only exception is where they are hedged against the cold. To the men, the tract is somewhat more benign and sustaining, but hardly with regard to their outward appearance. For they are sharp featured and unsightly in form. They are all fierce and numerous, and they greatly multiply. Few rivers carry to the sea, except the Hebrus, the Neston and the Strymon. The mountains at the interior are Haemon, Rhodope and

dopē & orbelon ſacris liberi patris & cœtu menadum or
pheo primū initiante celebratos:equis hæmus in tantū al
titudinis abit:ut euxinū & adriā ex ſūmo uertice oſtendat.
una gens traces habitant aliis aliiſque præditi & nomini
bus & moribus qdā feri ſunt & ad mortē paratiſſimi. Ge
tæ utiq̃.Id uaria opinio perficit.Alii redituras putant ani·
mas obeuntiū.Alii & ſi nọn redeant non extingui tamen
ſed ad beatiora trāſire.Alii emori quidē: ſed id melius eē
quā uiuere.Itaq̃ lugentur apud quoſdam puerperia:natiq̃
deflentur.Funera contra feſta ſunt:&ueluti ſacra cantu lu
ſuque celebrantur.Ne fœminis quidem ſegnis eſt animus
ſuper mortuorū uirorū corpora iterfici:ſimulq̃ ſepeliri uo
tū eximiū habent:& quia plures ſimul ſingulis nuptæ ſunt
cuius id ſit decus apud iudicaturos magno certamine affe
ctant:moribus datur:eſtque maxime lætū.cū in hoc con
tenditur: uincere.Mœrent alii uocibus: & cū acerbiſſimis
planctibus efferunt.At quibus conſolari eos animus eſt ar
ma opeſque ad rogos deferunt:paratiq̃:ut dictitant.Cum
fato racētis:ſidetur in manus:uel paciſci uel decernere: ubi
nec pugnæ nec pecuniæ locus ſit:manentq̃dominos pro
ci.Nupturæ uirgines non a parentibus uiris traduntur: ſed
publice aut locantur ducendæ :aut uenerunt. Vtrum fiat
ex ſpecie & moribus cauſa eſt.Probæ formoſæq̃ in pre
cio ſunt:cæteras q̃ habeant mercede quæruntur.Vini uſus
quibuſdam ignotus eſt.Epulantibus tamen ubi ſup ignes
quos circūſident.quædā ſemina igeſta ſunt: ſimilis ebrie
tati hilaritas ex nidore contingit.In littoribus Iſtro proxi

Mount Orbelos; these are held sacred to the fatherland and to the covenant of the Maenads - the ones who were first initiated into the celebrations of Orpheus. Among the heights, Haemon rises to the greatest altitude, so that from the summit of its peak even the Euxine Sea and the Adriatic Sea may be seen. Only one clan from the Thracians inhabits this region, but the tribe is known by various names, and they have various ways. Some are entirely wild, and perfectly willing to die; these are the Getae, whose reputation is known to many. Some of them believe that the soul returns to the body once again. But some of them believe that it dies indeed, yet it passes on to live in a better state. Still others believe that to die is better than to live. Therefore, among them there is sorrowing at the birth of a child, and lamentation at its nativity. In contrast, a funeral is a matter of rejoicing, and then they sing and play in celebration. Neither are the souls of the women slack to accept death with their husband's bodies, and, similarly, wish to be buried along with them. Because a man may marry a number of wives, it is deemed fit that those surviving him should plead with judges that one might be awarded the joyous victory of death. Weeping and wailing by all the others follows the decision granted to the chosen one; the rest are left to cry and mourn. But those who would seek to give them consolation of soul, bring forth their weapons and their wealth. They ask that they themselves might be carried also, as being prepared for death. With prostrations and with faithful hands, they pledge peace and understanding toward that place where there shall be neither money nor conflict. At their nuptials, the virgins are not given to the man by their parents, but are either publicly auctioned for marriage, or they are sold. Whether it may be caused by their beauty or by their manners, the greatest price is assigned to the most attractive. The others may quest to have marriage by means of their own dowry. The use of wine, for some of them, is unknown. But in feasting, they gather around a fire, and cast into the flames a certain type of seed. From the fumes, they seem inebriated and hilarious. At the shoreline, the river, Ister, is in proximity

ma ẽ Iſtropolis. Deǐde a Mileſiis deducta calatis:& Trito
nice:& portus caria:&Tiriſtris promontorium:quod præ
teruectos alter ponti angulus accipit:aduerſus Phaſiaco:&
niſi amplior foret:ſimilis fuit.Hic bizone motu terræ in/
tercidit.Eſt portus crunos:urbes dionyſiopolis.Oddeſſos
Meſſembria.Anchialos & intimo in ſinu atque ubi pon/
tus alterũ ſui flexũ angulo finit magna Apollonia:recta de
hinc ora:niſi cp media ferme in promontoriũ:quod thin
niã uocant:exit & incuruis contra ſe littoribus obtenditur
urbeſcp ſuſtinet Halmydeſon & philiã & phinopoli.Ha/
ctenus pontus.Deinde eſt boſphorus & propontis.In boſ
phoro Bizantiũ.In propontide Selymbria:perinthus ba/
thynis.Amoeſque:qui interfluunt erginus & atyras. Tum
Rheſo regnata quondã pars thraciæ & biſantæ ſamiorũ:
& ingens aliquando cypſela.Poſt locus: quẽ grai macron
tichos appellãt:& in radice magnæ peninſulæ ſedens lyſi
machia.Terra:quæ ſequitur nuſquã lata atcphic arctiſſima
inter helleſpontũ ægeucp procurrit. Anguſtias Iſthmon.
frontẽ ǎius maſtuſiã:totã cherſoneũ appellant.Ob multa
memorabile eſt.In ea flumen ægos naufragio claſſis atti/
cæ inſigne. Eſt & Abydo obiacens ſeſtos Leandri amore
pernobilis.Eſt & regio:in qua perſarum exercitus diuiſas
ſpacio pelagocp terras auſus pontibus iungere;mirũ atque
ingens facinus:ex Aſia in græciam pedes & non nauigata
maria tranſgreſſus eſt.Sunt Protheſilai oſſa conſecrata de
lubro.Eſt & portus Cœlos athenienſibus & lacedæmo/
nii naualis acie decernentibus laconicæ claſſis ſignatus ex/

to the city of Istropolis. Beyond this location, the Milesians once built the towns of Calatis and Tritonice, along with the port city of Caria at the promontory, Tiristris. The landmass here acts as one of the headlands at the narrows leading into the sea, and at the reverse side lies Phasis - the one is similar, if wider, than the other. It was here that the city, Bizone, was destroyed during an earthquake. Here, too, is the port Crunos, and the cities, Dionysiopolis, Odessus and Messembria. Anchialos stands at the innermost part of the bay by the place where the sea again curves to meet that great city, Apollonia. At this point the bay runs out nearly straight, and its center passes a promontory named Thinnia. With sharp bends, the coast follows a reversing line so far as the towns, Halmydeson, Phila and Phinopoli. Here is found Pontus, then the Bosphorus, then Propontis. At the Bosphorus is the town Bizantium, and at Propontis are the cities Selymbria, Perinthus, Bathynis and Amoes, with the placid streams, Erginus and Atyras flowing through them. Rhesus, at one time, had exercised rule over this part of Thrace, including Bisanthe, which the Samians had, and the city of Cypsela. Past this location is the place which, to the Greeks is known as Macrontichos, and then, at the stem of the great peninsula, is sited Lysimachia. The land which is then sequential is nowhere wide spread, but runs in a narrow formation until it finally carries between the Hellespont and the Aegean Sea. The strait here is the Isthmus - at the front of which is Mastusia, but the entire peninsula is the Chersoneses. Much memorabilia is here. In the river, Aegos, was the signal defeat of the Attic fleet. Then is Abydos, lying by Sestos, which was made noble through the loving devotion of Leander. Then is the region in which the Persian army, at the dividing space between the seas, dared to join them by bridges. Miraculous and ingenious was this fabrication: out of Asia and into Greece they advanced on foot, and were not transferred by ship across the sea. Here the bones of Protesilaus are consecrated by a shrine. Here is the port Coelos, where the Athenians and the Lacedemonians fought a great sea battle, resulting in the complete destruction of the Lacedemonian fleet.

cido.Eft cynoffema tumulus hecubæ fiue ex figura cãis in quam conuerfa traditur:fiue ex fortũa:in quam deciderat humili nomine excepto.Eft macidos.Eft helleus:quæ fi/ nit hellefpontum.Aegeum ftatim pelagus uafte longum littus impellit:fummotafque terras hinc ad promontoriũ quod Sunium uocatur:magno ambitu'mollique circũagit eius tractum legentibus præuectifque maftufiã tum finus intrandus eft:qui alterum chefonefi latus abluens iugo fa/ cile uallis includitur & ex fluuio: quem accipit. Melas di/ ctus.Duas urbes amplectit'alopeconefum & altero Ifthmi littoris fitã cardiã. Eximia é ænos ab Aenea profugo con/ dita.Circa hebrum cicones. Tranfeundem dorifcos: ubi Xerxé copias fuas:quia numero non poterat:fpatio men/ fum ferunt.Deinde promontorium Serrium:ex quo ca/ nentem orphea fecuta & narrantur nemora.Zonæ. Tum fcenos fluuius:& ripis eius adiacens maronia.Regio ulte/ rior Diomedem tulit immanibus equis mãdendos folitũ obiectare aduenas:& iifdem ab Hercule obiectum. Tur/ ris:quam Diomedis uocat: fignũ fabulæ remanet:& urbs: quam foror eius fuo nomine nominauit. Abdere: fed ea magis id memorandum habet q̃ Democritum phyficum tulit quã q̃ ita condita eft:Vltra neftos fluit.Interque eum & ftrymona urbes funt: Philippi. Apollonia. Amphipo/ lis.Inter ftrymona & Athon turris calarnea & portus ca/ prullon.urbs acanthos & Oefyma.inter athon & pallene ncleona & olynthos. Strimon : ficut diximus: amnis eft longeque ortus & tenuis:alienis fubinde aquis fit amplior

Here is Cynossema (the hound's head), and the grave of Queen Hecuba - the place having acquired such a name either from the image of a dog where she was interred, or possibly from the humble fate which befell her. Here are Macidos and Helleus, which form the terminus of the Hellespont. The Aegean Sea stands here - coursing vast and far by the shorelands until it reaches the promontory called Sunium. Those who circumnavigate beyond this great ambit proceed past Mastusia into a bay. This leads on the one side to Chersonesus - the shore being formed as though a valley - and, on the other side, to a river called the Melas. It embraces two towns: Alopeconesus, located by the one shore of the Isthmus, and Cardia, located by the other. The city Aenos is esteemed for having been built by Aeneas during his retreat. Around the river Hebrus are the Cicones people. Passing beyond here is Doriscos, at which place Xerxes, the king, assembled his forces, and, being unable to count their huge numbers, he measured them against the entire stretch of the landmass. Thence after is the promontory of Serrium. From its forest grove at Zona, all are said to have followed after Orpheus when he began to sing. After this comes the river, Scenos, and the adjacent watercourse, the Maronia. The kingdom beyond it was held by Diomedes, who caused strangers to be carried out as fodder for his wild horses. Yet he himself was thrown to them by Hercules. The turret which is named for Diomedes remains there as a sign of this fable, in addition to the city which his sister had named for herself, Abdera. Nonetheless, the city has a more fit memorial than such things as these; it was the birthplace of the natural philosopher, Democritus. The Nestos flows past here, and, beside it, is the Strymon, both of which water the towns Philippi, Apollonia and Amphipolis. Between the Strymon River and Mount Athos stands the turret Calarne and the port Caprullon, with the cities Acanthos and Oesyma. Found between Athos and Pallene are the villages of Cleone and Olynthos. The Strymon, as we have mentioned, runs at great length from its source as a narrow watercourse, but, directly, it is magnified by other streams,

Liber Secundus.

& ubi non longe a mari lacum fecit: maiore quã uenerat
alueo erumpit. Athos mons eſt adeo elatus: ut credatur al
tius atiem quã unde imbres cadunt ſurgere. Capit opinio
fidem: quia de aris quas in uertice ſuſtinet: non abluitur ci
nis: ſed quo relinquitur aggere manet. Cæterum non pro
montorio: ut alii: uerum totus eſt: totoque longe dorſo p
cedit in pelagus. Q ua continenti adhæret & Xerxe i gra
ios tendente perfoſſus trãſnauigatuſque: & actus freto na
uigabili peruius. Ima eius tenent paruæ pelaſgorum colo
niæ. In ſummo fuit oppidum Acroathon: in quo ut fe
runt: dimidio longior quã in aliis terris ætas habitantium
erat. Palene ſoli tam patentis: ut in quinque urbium ſe
des ſit atque ager. Tota in altũ abit. Anguſta ſatis unde in
cipit. Ibi eſt potidæa: at ubi laxius patet. Mende Scioneq;
referẽdæ illa ab hæretris. Hæc ab Achiuis: capto Ilio reme
antibus poſita. Tum Macedonũ populi. quot urbes habi
tant: quarum Pellam maxime illuſtrem alumni efficiunt.
Philippus græciæ domitor: Alexander etiam aſiæ. In litto
re flexus megibernæus inter promontoria diuidit canaſtre
um & portum: qui copos dicitur. Vrbes toronen & phy
ſcellam atque unde ipſi nomen eſt. Megibernam incingit
Caneſtrio promontorio Scione proxima eſt. Mecyberne
us aũt.i. ſinus in medio qua terra dat gremiũ: medice i lit
tora igredit. Cæterũ lõgis i altũ imiſſis lateribus igens iter
maria ſinus eſt. in eũ axius per macedonas ẽt per theſſalos
Peneus excurrit ante axiũ theſſalonice eſt. inter utrunque
Caſſandria, Cydna aloros derris a Peneo ſepias corinthia.

and, at a place not far from the sea, it forms a lake, and the channel then rushes more quickly forward. Mount Athos - so great in its elevation - is believed to surge up even to where the rains fall. The opinion is held as a truth because from the altars that have been set up on its summit, the votive ashes are never rinsed away, but instead, they remain just as they had been accumulated. Unlike the other promontories, this one, indeed, projects itself toward the sea, but along the entire length of its great back ridge. At the place where it adheres into the land mass of the continent proper, it had been cut completely across by Xerxes for the invasion of Greece. He then cross-navigated it through this narrow canal. The peninsula's lower tip is held by a few small Pelasgian colonies. At its upper sector is found the city of Acroathon, in which - so the story carries - the inhabitant might live half again the length of the normal life span. Palene carries so much foliage that five cities, in addition to all their fields, are supported there. The whole of it is sited on rising ground. Yet its initial point is on a narrow land spit. Here is the town of Potidaea: but inherent to that place, where the land spreads wide, are the cities of Mende and Scione, and they are still thus called by the present inheritors. Both had been founded by the Achaeans on their return from the capture of Ilium. Then come the Macedonian people. Regarding the cities which they inhabit, Pella is the most illustrious. Among its alumni, are to be noted both Philip of Macedonia, conqueror of Greece, and his son, Alexander the Great, conqueror of Asia. The sea line forms an inlet at Megibernaus which divides the promontory of Canastreum from the port called Copos. Enclosed within are the towns Torone, Physcellam and Megiberna, and by this last name it is known. The bay Mergibernaus touches the promontory Canestrium, with Scione in near proximity. Then Megibernaus, in the midst of the land mass, takes a lap-like shape, and partly enters a bay. The remainder extends at length, and carries, as a gulf, to the sea. In it, flow the rivers Axius, from Macedonia, and Peneus, from Thessaly. By the Axius is Thessalonica, Cassandria, Cydna, Aloros and Derris. By the Peneus, are Sepias, Corinthia,

melibœa.cıſtanea pares ad famã:niſi ꝗ philotedes alum
nus Melibœã illuminat.Terrę interiores claris locorũ no╱
minibus inſignes pene nihil ignobile ferunt.Hinc nõ lõ
ge eſt Olympus.hic pelion.hic oſſa:montes gigantum fa
bula belloꝗ memorati.Hic muſarũ parens domuſꝗ pie╱
ria.hic nouiſſime calcatũ graio Herculi ſolũ ſaltus œtæus.
hic ſacro nemore nobilia tẽpe.hic libetrha carminũꝗ fon
tes obiacẽt.Tum iã uaſte & multũ prominẽs græcia: & dũ
myrthoũ pelagus attingat:a ſeptẽtrione in meridiem ue╱
da:qua ſol oritur ægeis:qua occidit Ioniis fludibus obia╱
cet:ac proxime ſpacioſa: & hellas nomine grandi fronte
procedit:mox mari utroꝗ & Ionio magis latere eias ítran
te donec quinꝗ milia paſſuũ pateat media ferme prope i╱
ciditur.Deíde rurſum terris huc ſe & illuc uerũ in Ionium
mare magis expandentibus progreſſiſꝗ in altũ non tam
lata ꝗ cœperat:igens tamen iterũ & quaſi peninſula exten
ditur:uocaturꝗ peloponneſos:ob ſinus & promontoria:
quis ut fibris littora eius inciſa ſunt:ſimul ꝗ tenui tramite
in latus effunditur: platani folio ſimillima.In macedonia
prima eſt Theſſalia.Deinde magneſia.phthiotis.doris.lo
cris.phocis.boetis.attis.megaris.Sed omnium attis clariſ
ſima.In peloponneſo argolis.Laconice.meſſenia.achaia.
elis.arcadia.ultra ætolia.arcanania.epiros uſꝗ in adriam.
De locis atꝗ urbibus:quæ mare non abluit hæc maxime
memoranda ſunt in theſſalia.Lariſſa aliquando iolcos.id
eſt Magneſia Antronia. In phthiotide phthia.In locride
cynos & callicros.In phocide delphi & mons parnaſus:&

Meliboea and Castanea, all of them equally famed, except that it was the Greek hero Philoctetes - an alumnus of Meliboea - who had made the place so luminous. Toward the interior of the country are found the names of many classical locations, and only a very few of them are found to be insignificant. Not far to the interior are Mount Olympus, Mount Pelion and Mount Ossa: all great heights and all memorialized in the fables of war. Here is the dwelling of the Muses, in their parents' home, at Pieria. Here is the final treading place of Hercules, the Greek, and the mountain where he, at last, set foot upon the grove at Oetaeus. Here is the sacred valley of noble Tempe. Here is Libethra, and the song emitted from its fountains. Thence come the numerous and vast promontories of Greece, running from the Myrthoan Sea toward the north and south, as on a vector. The sun rises upon the Aegean Sea, and it sets below the waves of the Ionian Sea. In its proximity are the broad spaces of the land named Hellas. Its grand frontal mass is thrust forward, only to be cut nearly through by the seas, and by the intrusion of the Ionian waters, which reduce the land neck to no more than five miles across. Then the landfall, reversing itself, expands laterally into the deep toward the Ionian Sea. Next, the country spreads, but less widely so, and extends to take on a peninsula-like form. This configuration is called the Peloponnese. On account of all the bays and promontories by which the shore line is fragmented, it bears a similarity to the cross-foliation of the plane tree. In Macedonia, to begin with, is the area of Thessaly. Following thereafter is Magnesia, Phthiotis, Doris, Locris, Phocis, Boetis, Attis and Megaris. But of them all, Attis is pre-eminent. Within the Peloponnese are Argolis, Laconice, Messenia, Achaia, Elis and Arcadia. Beyond are Aetolia, Arcanania and Epiros, even to the Adriatic Sea. Of those locations and cities which are not washed by the sea, the most memorable in Thessaly is Larissa (once called Iolcos) - in Magnesia it is Antronia - in Phthiotis it is Phthia - in Locris it is Cynos and Callicros - in Phocis it is Delphi and Mount Parnasus and

Liber Secundus.

Apollinis fanū atqʒ oraculū.In Boetia thebæ.& citheron
fabulis carminibuſqʒ celeberrimus.In attide eleuſin Cere∕
ri conſecrata & clariores: q̄ ut indicari egeant.Athenæ. In
megaride unde regioni nomen eſt megara.Vt in argolide
argos & mycenæ & templū iunonis uetuſtate & religione
pcelebre.In laconide terapne. Lacedæmon. amyclæ mōs
Taygetus.In meſſenia Meſſene &methone.In achaia atqʒ
elide quondā piſæ œnomai.elis & numē delubrūqʒ olym
pii Iouis certamine gymnico & ſingulari ſanctitate. Ipſo
quidem tamen ſimulacro:quod phidiæ opus eſt maxime
nohile.Arcadiam peloponneſiacæ gentes undiqʒ incin∕
gunt. In ea ſunt urbes pſophis & Tenia.orchomenos.mō
tes Pholoe. Cyllenius.Parthenius.mænalus.flumina ery∕
manthus & ladon. In ætolia naupactos.In acarnania Stra
tos oppida. In epiro dodonæi iouis tēplum & fons ideo
ſacer:qʒ cum ſit frigidus: & immerſas faces ſicut cæteri ex∕
tinguat:ubi ſine igne procul admouentur accendit. At cū
littora leguntur a promontorio Sepiade per Demetriam
& boion & pteleon & echinō ad pagaſ cum ſinum curſus
eſt:ille urbem pagaſam amplexus amnem Sperchion acci
pit:& quia Minyæ colchida petentes inde argo nauem ſol
uere memorantur. Ab eo ad ſunium tendentibus illa præ∕
nauiganda.maliacus & opuntius grandes ſinus:& in iis cæ
ſorum etiam laconum trophæa Thermopylæ Opes ſcar∕
phia enemides alope.Antedon.larumnæ.aulis agamem∕
noniæ graiorumqʒ claſſis in troiam coniurantium ſtatio.
Marathon magnarum multarummqʒ uirtutum teſtis iam

the temple of Apollo with its oracle - in Boeotia it is Thebes and Citheron, celebrated in fables and songs - in Attis it is Eleusis, consecrated to Ceres. Yet, for the greatest beauty and clarity, one must indicate only Athens itself. In Megara it is the city of Megara, by which the region is named. In Argolis it is Argos and Mycenae, along with the temple of Juno, venerated in its ancient religious celebrations. In Laconice it is Terapne, Lacedaemon and Amyclae, with Mount Taygetus. In Messenia it is Mesene and Methone. In Achaia and in Elis (once called Pisae) it is Oenomaius, but in Elis it is the shrine of the Olympian Jove, and its gymnastic contests, and also famed for its singular sanctity. This itself is renowned for the statue which was the crowning work of Phidias, the greatest sculptor. Arcadia is everywhere cinctured about by all the nations of the Peloponnese. Within itself, however, are the cities of Psophis, Tenia, and Orchomenos. Its mountains are Pholoe, Cyllenius, Parthenius and Maenalus. Its rivers are the Erymanthus and the Ladon. In Aetolia, it is the city Naupactos. In Acarnania, it is the city of Stratos. In Epirus, it is the Dodonic temple of Jove. Also, a fountain here is held sacred; in itself it is frigid, and should any torches be immersed in it they are, as in any other fountain, extinguished. However, should the torches, unlighted, be removed a great way off, they are ignited. Those who have studied this shoreline, read it from the promontory of Sepias through Demetrias and Boion, Pteleon and Echinon to the curve of the bay Pagasa. Herein is the city of Pegasae, embraced by the river Sperchion. Only because the clan of the Minyae -when they sought to go to Colchis, and sailed in the ship Argo - is the place held in memory. From it, all those who would stretch sail for Sunium must trans-navigate past here. Here, too, are Maliacus and Opuntius, the grand harbors, and in them are found the carved images of the Lacedaemonians who were slain at Thermopylae. Seen here are Opes, Scarphia, Enemides, Alope, Antedon and Larumnae. It was in the port, Aulis, that Agamemnon, along with the Greek sea fleet which conspired against Troy, had been stationed. Marathon, testifying to many great deeds of heroism - even

Pomponii Melæ.

inde a Thefeo perfica maxima clade pernotus. Ramnus
parua illuftris tamé:q̃ in ea fanū eft Amphiarai:& phidia
ca nemefis.Thoricos & brauronion olim urbes:iam tan/
tum nomina.Sunium promontorium eft:finitq̃ id littus
hellados:quod fpectat ad orientem.Inde ad meridié ter/
ra conuertitur ufq̃ ad megaram:atticæ ut modo latere:ita
nunc fronte pelago adiacens.Ibi eft Pyræus atheniefium
portus.Scyronia faxa fæuo quondam fcyronis hofpitio ét
nunc infamia.Megarenfium tractus Ifthmon attingit.
Hoc illi cognomen eft:quia quinque milium fpacio æge
um mare ab ionio fubmouens angufto tramite helladi pe
loponnefon annectit.In eo eft oppidum Cenchreæ fanū
Neptuni. Ludi quos ifthmicos uocant:celebres: corithos
olim clara opib9.Poft clade notior.Nūc romana colonia
Ex fumma arce:quã acrocorinthon appellãt:maria utraq̃
contuens.Peloponnéfi oram:ficut diximus:finus & pro/
montoria lacerant.Ab oriente Bucephalos & cherfonefus
& fcyleon:ad meridié malea. tænaros. achritas: Icthis. ad
uefperum chelonates & araxos. Habitant ab Ifthmo ad
fcyleon epidaurii æfculapii templo inclyti & troezenii fi/
de focietatis articæ illuftres.Portus Sarronicus & fchœni/
tas & pagonus.Oppida autē Epidaurus & troezen & her/
miona his littoribus appofita funt:Inter fcyleon & ma//
leam laconicus.Inter tænaron & acritam & ichthym cypa
rifius .In argolico funt noti amnes erafinus atq̃ inachus:
& notum oppidum lerne. In laconico cythius &curotas in
ipfo tænaro Neptunni templum & fpecus illi:quē in pōto

to those of Theseus - is most widely famed for the defeat of the Persians. Ramnus, a small but illustrious town, contains in it the temple of Amphiaraeus and, through the art of Phidias, the image of the goddess, Nemesis. Thoricos and Brauronion, in times of old, were cities: now, however, no more than names. Sunium is a promontory; it is the limit and shoreline of Hellas which looks toward the east. Thereafter the land reverts toward the south, even to Megara. Attica, positioned near the shoreline, then faces adjacent to the front of the sea. Here is Pyraeus, the Athenian port. The jagged Scyronian rocks along here were well known to the ruler, Scyron and to his unfortunate guests, and even now they are held in infamy. The tract of Megaris is contingent to the Isthmus. This is its proper name, for within a space of no more than five miles, it divides the Aegean Sea from the Ionian Sea. The narrow neck then conjoins Hellas to the Peloponnese. In this place is the city of Cenchrea, and the temple of Neptune. The games, which are referred to as the Isthmian games, are celebrated here. Corinth, in ancient days, was a great city. Afterward, however, it was more widely noted for its total destruction. Now it is a Roman colony. From the summit of its tower, which is called Acrocorinth, both the seas together may be seen. The Peloponnesian shore, as we have stated, is laced with inlets and promontories. To the east is Bucephalos, Chersonesus and Scyleon: to the south is Malea, Taenaros, Achritas and Icthis: to the west is Chelonates and Araxos. The inhabitants from the Isthmus to Scyleon are the Epidaurians, along with their famed temple of Aesculapius. The Troezenians, on account of their faithful association with the Athenians, have been made illustrious. Here is the bay Sarronicus, with Schoenicus and Pagonus. The towns, however, of Epidaurus, Troezen and Hermion are positioned along this shore. Between Scyleon and Malea is the land of Laconia. Between Taenaros, Achritas and Icthis is Cyparisius. In Argolis there are the notable rivers Erasinus and Inachus, with the famed city of Lerne. In Laconia, will be seen the isle, Cythius, and the stream, Eurotas. In Taenaros itself is the temple of Neptune and its cavern, which, being in Pontus,

Acherufium diximus:facie & fabula fimilis.In afineo flumen pamifum.In cyparifio alpheus. Nomé dedit urbs in
littore fita.Hic cyparifus.illinc afine.Meffenii pilliquc ter
ras colunt:& ipfa pelago pylos adiacet.Cyllene: calipolis.
patræ oram illam tenent:in quam Chelonatas & Araxos
excurrunt.Sed cyllenæ:ꝗ Mercurium ibi natum arbitran ·
tur infignis.Rhion deide:maris id nomen eft: angufte &
uelut freto lacus ore frequenti incidens inter ætolos & pe
loponefiacos ufque ad ifthmon irrumpit.In eo ad septen
trionem fpectare littora incipiunt.In his eft ægeon & ægi
na & Olyros & ficyon.ac in aduerfis pagæ: creufis. Anti-
cyra.œanthia.Cyrra:& notior aliquanto nomine calydõ
& euenos. Extrarhion in acarnania maxime clara funt op
pidum Leucas.flumen achelous.In epiro nihil ambracio
finu nobilius eft.Facit finus:qui anguftis faucibus & quæ
minus mille paffibus pateant grande pelagus admittit. Fa
ciunt urbes:quæ affident Actiũ.Argi.Amphilocis.Ambra
cia.æacidarum regna.Pyrrhiꝗ. Butroton ultra eft.Dein-
de Cerauni montes.ab iis flexus in adriam.hoc mare magnum fucceffu littorum acceptum : & uafte quidem in
latitudinem patens : qua penetrat tamen uaftius illyri-
cis ufque tergeftum cætera gallicis italifque gentibus cin-
guntur.Parthenii & dafarctæ prima eius tenent. Sequétia
paulatim Enthellæ:phæaces. Deinde funt : quos proprie
illyricos uocant.Tum pyræi & liburni & Iftria.Vrbiũ pri
ma eft Oricum.fecunda durachium Epidannos ante erat.
Romani nomé mutauere:qa uelut i dãnũ ituris omé id ui

we speak of by the name of Acherusium and, thereby, is tied to its connection with myth -
but we have always claimed that such things are based only on fancy and fable. In Asine
is the river Pamisum. In Cyparisus it is the river Alpheus. The names have been given
to the cities by the shoreline: the near, Cyparisus and the far, Asine. The Messenians and
the Pylians live here, with the tract of Pylos itself adjacent to the sea, and the cities Cyllene
and Calipolis. Patrae is set by the sea, at the place where the rivers Chelonatas and Araxos
flow outward. However, Cyllene is thought to be the place where Mercury was born.
Rhion then follows, which is named for the sea. Constricted, and similar to the mouth of
a lake, it falls between Aetolia and the Peloponnese, and breaks out at the Isthmus. In this
place the landform begins to look toward the north. Here are located: Aegeon, Aegina,
Olyros and Sicyon; but on the shore opposite to them are found the districts; Creusis,
Anticyra, Oeanthia, Cyrra and - that which is widely known by the name, Calydon - and
the river, Evenus. Other than Rhion in Arcarnania, the greatest city is Leucas, on the
stream, Achelous. In Epirus, nothing except the bay of Ambracio is noteworthy. This bay
is formed as a narrow throat, not a mile across, but it admits in the open sea. Cities are
found here: Actium and Argos, which were settled by Amphilocis. At Ambracia is the
kingdom of the Aecideans, and nearby is Pyrrhus. The city Butroton is beyond. Thence
after are the Ceraunian mountains, which follow their flexing path toward the Adriatic.
This sea, penetrating far into the shoreline, opens vast and wide and carries even to the
stretches of Illyria, so far as Tergestum. Its remainder then cinctures the nations of Gaul
and Italy. The Parthenians and the Dasarctae hold its first part, and, in sequence, the
lesser part is held by the Enthellae and the Phaeaces. Following are all those who are
properly called Illyrians. Then come the Pyreans, the Liburnians and the Istrians. The
primary city is Oricum, and then is Dyrrhachium. It had been Epidamnus before, but the
Romans changed the name. To them, it seemed an ill omen. They read *epidamnus* as
epidemic.

sum est. Vltra sunt appollonia:salona.iadera.nona. tragu
rium:sinus polaticus & pola quondam a colchis:ut ferunt
habitata:inquantum res transeunt nunc romana colonia
Amnes aũt æas:& nar.& danubius:qui iam dictus est ister
sed æas secundum apolloniã.Nar iter pyræos & liburnos:
per istros ister emittitur.Tergeste intimo in sinu adriæ situ
finit illyricum.

DE Italia magis qa ordo exigit q̃ qa mõstrari eget
pauca dicentur.Nota sunt omnia:ab alpibus inci
pit in altum excedere atque ut procedit se media
perpetuo apœnini iugo montis attollens inter adriacũ &
tuscum:siue ut alter eadem appellantur:inter superum ma
re & inferum excurrit diu solida.Verum ubi longe abit in
duo cornua scinditur:respicitque altero siculum pelagus:
altero ioniũm tota angusta & alicubi multo q̃ unde cœpit
angustior.Interiora eius aliæ aliæq̃ gentes.Sinistram par
tem Carni.& Veneti colunt togatam galliam.Tum italici
populi picentes.Frentani.Daũni.Apuli.Calabri.Salenti
ni.Ad dextrã sunt sub alpibus Ligures.Sub apœnino He
truria.post latium.Volsci.Campani.& super Lũcaniã Bru
tii.Vrbium:quæ procul a mari habitantur opulentissimæ
sunt ad sinistram Patauium Antenoris.Mutina & Bono
nia Romanorum coloniæ.Ad dextram Capua a Tuscis &
Roma quondam a pastoribus condita.Nunc si pro mate
ria dicatur alterum opus.At in oris proxima est a tergeste
Concordia.Interfluit Timauus nouem capitibus exurgens
uno ostio emissus.Deinde Natiso nõ longe a mari ditem

Beyond are found Apollonia, Salona, Iadera, Nona and Tragurium. The bay of Pola and the town of Pola - at one time inhabited by the Colchians - was transferred, for various causes, to be a colony of the Romans. The streams, however, are the Aeas, the Nar and the Danube, already spoken of as the river Ister. But the Aeas flows toward the Apollonians; the Nar between the Pyreans and the Liburnians; the Ister toward the Istrians. Tergeste, innermost on the Adriatic bay, is sited at the border of Illyria.

Of Italy, the order of procedure here will require some demonstration, but not a great deal of it needs explanation - it is known to one and all. From the initial heights of the Alps, as they rise ever higher toward the middle of their perpetual cresting, the Apennines carry forward between the Adriatic and the Tuscan Seas - otherwise called the upper sea and the lower. For a great distance they are thus massed. Yet, at last, they are split apart in the manner of two horns. The one faces over the sea of Sicily, and the other over the Ionian. In its entirety, it is narrow, but at certain places it is even more constricted than at its beginning. Its interior contains several nations. To the left side are the Carnians and the Venetians, those people who adopted the toga along the border of Gaul. Thereafter are the Italian peoples: the Picentians, the Frentanians, the Daunians, the Apulians, the Calabrians and the Salentians. To the right side below the Alps, are the Ligurians and, below the Apennines, are the Etrurians. After are the Latini, the Volsci, the Campani and, above Lucania, are the Brutians. Of the cities which lie far from the sea, the richest, on the left side, is the town of Padua, founded by Antenor. Mutina and Bononia are Roman colonies. On the right side is Capua, founded by the Tuscans, and Rome, founded by shepherds long ago - but now grown so great that it possesses enough material for the writing of yet another opus. In proximity to the sea is Tergeste and Concordia. Flowing between is the river Timavus, surging out of nine springs into one stream. Thence is the river, Natiso, not far from the sea,

attingit Aquileiam. Vltra eft altinum. Superiora late occu
pat littora padus. Nanq; ab imis radicibus uefculi montis
exortus paruis fe primum fontibus colligit:& aliquatenus
exilis ac macer:mox aliis amnibus adeo augefcit atque ali
tur:ut fe per feptem ad poftremum oftia effundat. Vnum
de his magnum padum appellant. Inde tam citus profilit.
ut difcuffis fluctibus diu qualem emifit: undam agat:fu
umque etiam in mari alueum feruet: donec eũ ex aduerfo
littore iftriæ eodem impetu profluens ifter amnis excipiat
Hac re per ea loca nauigantibus:qua utrinq; amnes eunt
inter marinas aquas dulcium hauftus eft. A pado ad An
conam tranfitur Rauenna. Ariminum. Pifaurum. Fane
ftris colonia. flumen metaurus atque Efis: & illa in angu
fto illorum duorum promontoriorum ex diuerfo coeun
tium inflexi cubiti imagine fedés:& ideo a grais picta An
cona. Inter gallicas italicafq; gentes quafi terminus inter
eft. Hæc enim prægreffos Piceni littora excipiunt. In qui
bus humana potentia. cliterna. cupra urbes. caftella autem
firmum. adria. truentinum. Id ei fluuio: qui præterit no
men eft. Ab eo. Senogallia maritima: Habent enim flumi
nis hoftia urbes bucara & hiftonium. Dauni autem Tifer
num amnem. Claterniam. Lucrinum. Theanum oppida
montemq; garganum. Sinus eft continuo Apulo littore
incinctus nomine Vrias modicus fpatio: pleraq; afper ac
ceffu. extra Sypuntu:uel ut graii dixere Sipyus:& flumen:
quod canufium attingens:aufidum appellant. Poft Bari
um & Egnatia & Ennio ciue nobiles rudiæ: & in calabria

and touching the rich city of Aquileia. Past here is the town of Altinum. The upper side is occupied by the broad river plain of the Po. Indeed, its tributaries flow from the base of Mount Vesulus, collecting at the first spring, it courses for a time weak and thin, but soon increasing itself by other springs, it runs at last into a delta of seven outlets at its mouth. Only one of them is referred to as the great Po. It rushes forth so quickly that it disperses the tides by the force of its surge. The sea is carried by the river's flood until, at last, from the opposite shore, the Ister joins the surge with the might of its own channel. Throughout the length of these waters, navigators find themselves drawing up fresh water from the riverine current, even in the midst of the sea. From the Po to the port of Ancona, the way passes through Ravenna, Ariminum, Pisaurum and the colony of Fanestris, along the rivers Metaurus and Esis. These encircle the two promontories which isolate Ancona, and thereby create the image of a flexed elbow in the reclining position. And so it was that the Greeks thus pictured Ancona. Between the people of Gaul and Italy, it serves as a terminus for them. Those progressing through here come along the shore of Picene, in which are found the cities: Numana, Potentia, Cliterna and Cupra; and the castles: Firmum, Adria and Truentinum. By this is a river of the same name. From here is maritime Senogallia, having the stream Ostia, with the cities of Bucara and Histonium. But the Daunians, however, possess the river Tisernum and the towns of Claternia, Lucrinum, and Theanum, at Mount Garganum. The bay line is continuous here from Apulia, enclosing within the place which, for a short distance, is named for the town, Uria. Here, the sea access is difficult. Beyond is Sypuntum, or, as the Greeks call it, Sipyus, and the river touching Canusium, which they call the Aufidus. After which are the towns Barium and Egnatia - it was the poet, Ennius, who gave fame to the town, Rudiae. And in Calabria

Brundusium.Valetium lubiæ hydus mons.tum salentini
campi:& salentina littora: & urbs graia Gallipolis. Hu
cusque adria: Hucusque Italiæ latus alterum pertinet.
Frons eius in duo quidem se cornua sicut supra diximus
scindit.Cæterum mare:quod inter utraque admisit tenui
bus promontoriis semel iterumque distinguens non uno
margine circuit:nec diffusum patensque:sed per sinus re
cipit.Primus tarentinus dicitur inter promontoria.Salen
& lacinium.In eoq3 sunt Tarentus: methapontum. hera
clea.Croto.Turium.Secundus Scyllaceus inter promon
toria Lacinium & Zephyrium:in quo est Petilia. Cocin
thus.Scyllaceum mistræ.Tertius inter zephyrium & Bru
tium. Consentiam . Cauloniam: locrosque circundat. In
Brutio sunt colūna regia rhegium.Scylla.Taurianū & me
taurum.Hinc in tuscum mare deflexus est.& eiusdem ter
ræ latus alterum terina hippo nunc ūibon temesa. Căpe
tia.Blanda Buxentum.Velia.Palinurus olim phrygii gu
bernatoris.Nunc loci nomen.Pæstanus sinus.Pæstum op
pidum.Silarus amnis.Picentia.peræ: quas Syrenes habi
tauere.Mineruæ promontorium. Omnia Lucaniæ loca.
Sinus puteolanus.Surrentum.Herculanæū.Vesuuii mon
tis aspectus Pompeii.Neapolis.puteoli.Lacus lucrinus &
Auernus.Baiæ.Missenum.Id nunc loci aliquando phry
gii militis nomen.Cumæ.Linternum. Vulturnus amnis.
Vulturnum oppidum.Amœna căpaniæ littora. Sinuessa.
Liris.Minturnæ.Formiæ.fundi.Terracina.Cyrces domus
aliquando cyrceii.Antium.Aphrodisiū. Ardea. Laurētū

are Brundisium, Valetium, Lubiae and Mount Hydrus. Then come the plains of Salentini by the shoreline of Salentina, at the Greek town of Gallipoli. Here lies the Adriatic Sea, and, at this point, the limit to that side of Italy. Its front then splits in two, and so resembles paired horns, as has been said before. The sea remaining between them follows no singular path along an open shore, but arches through bays. First, comes Tarentum (so called) found between the promontories of Salen and Lacinium. Within them are: Tarentum, Methapontus, Heraclea, Croto and Turium. Then, second, the bay, Scyllaceus, between the promontories of Lacinium and Zephyrium, at which place are found the towns of Petilia, Cocinthus, Scyllaceum and Mistrae. Then, third, between Zephyrium and Brutium (within this area) are Consentia, Caulonia and Locri. In Brutium are the columns of the kingdom of Rhegium, with Scylla, Taurianum and Metaurum. Here is the Tuscan Sea at the place of its deflection, and, toward the land side, is Terina Hippo (now called Vibon), Temesa, Campetia, Blanda, Buxentum and Velia. Paulinurus, once helmsman to the Phrygians, is now only the name of a location. At the bay of Paestanus and its city of Paestrum, is the river Silarus. The town Picentia has its famous rocks, in which the Sirens (mermaids) dwelt by the promontory of Minerva. All of this is in the locale of Lucania, including the bay of Puteoli, Sorrento, Herculaneum, Mount Vesuvius overlooking Pompeii, Naples and Puteoli. Following are the lakes Lucrinus and Avernus, with the towns Baiae and Missenum. This is now only the name of a location, but at one time was named for one of the Phrygian military. Here are Cumae and Linternum, on the river Volturno and its castle, Volturno. Delightful is everything along the Campanian seaside - Sinuessa, Liris, Minturnae, Formiae, Fundi, Terracina, Circe's house (once called Circeii), Antium, Aphrodisium, Ardea, Laurentum and

oſtia citra Tyberim in hoc latere ſunt. Vltra pyrgi: anio:
caſtrum nouũ.Grauiſce Coſſa Telamon. Populonia. Ce
ẽna.Piſæ:hetruſca & loca & nomina.Deinde Luna Ligu
rum:& liguria:& Genua:& Sabatia: & Albigaunũ. Tum
paulon & Varum fiumina utraque ab alpibus delapſa:ſed
Varum:quia italiam finit aliquanto notius.Alpes ipſæ ab
iis littoribus longe lateqʒ diffuſæ: primo ad ſeptentrioné
magno gradu excurrunt.Deinde ubi germaniã attigerunt
uerſo impetu in orientem abeunt:dirreptiſqʒ populis ima
nibus uſqʒ in Thtaciam penetrant.

Allia Lemano lacu & gebennicis mótibus ĩ duo
latera diuiſa.atque altero tuſcum pelagus attin
gens:altero oceanum.Hinc a Varo illinc a Rhe
no ad pyreneum uſque promittitur.Pars noſtro mari ap
poſita:fuit aliquando braccata: nunc narbonenſis magis
culta & magis conſita:ideoqʒ etiã lætior. Vrbium:quas ha
bet:opulentiſſimæ ſunt uaſio uocuntiorũ.Vienna alobro
gum.auenio.cauarum arecomicorum.Nemauſus. Toloſſa
Tectoſagum ſecundanorum.Arauſio ſextanorũ:arelate:ſe
ptimanorumqʒ Blittera:ſed anteſtatonis atacinorum:de
cimanorumqʒ colonia.Vnde olim iis terris auxilium fuit:
nunc & nomen & decus eſt Martius narbo. In littoribus
aliquot ſunt cum aliquibus nominibus loca. Cæterum ra
ræ urbes:quia rari portus:& omnis plaga auſtro:atqʒ afri
co expoſita eſt. Nicæa tangit alpes:tangit oppidum decea
tũ:tãgit antipolis.Deide eſt forũ Iulii octauianorũ colo
nia:tũc poſt Athenopoli:& olbiã:& glanon & cithariſtes

Ostia, at the near side of the Tiber's bank. Beyond is Pyrgi, and the stream, Anio, and then the cities, Castrum Novum, Graviscae, Cossa, Telamon, Populonia, Cecina, Pisa - but Etruria is the general location and name for these. Then on is Luna (Ligurian), Liguria, Genoa, Sabatia and Albigaunum. Thereafter, the rivers Paulon and Varus fall from the Alps, but the Varus, being on the Italian border, is widely noted. The Alps, of themselves, range far and wide from this border, first toward the north, rising hugely in their course. Then, touching Germany, they turn to the east and extend further, penetrating many dreadful nations, even to the Thracians.

Gaul, in the area of Lake Lemanus and Mount Gebenna, is divided into two parts. Of these, one side touches the Tuscan Sea and the other touches the ocean. From there, at the Varus, it runs as far as the Rhine to the Pyrenees promontory. That part which is positioned toward our sea was called, at one time, Braccata, but now is Narbonne, and being more populous and cultivated now, it is an attractive area. Of the cities here: the most opulent is Vasio of the Vocontii, Vienna of the Allobrogians, Avenio of the Cavarians, Nemausus of the Arecomicians, Tolossa of the Tectosages, Arausio of the Secundanians, Arelate of the Sextanians and Blittera of the Septimani. Yet stationed long before any of them were the Atacinians, and their tenth-year, tithe-held land colony. Once, in times of old, all these lands had been given aid; now they have the name and the distinction of Martius Narbo. The sea coast has varied names at varied locales. The remainder, however, has few cities, and the sea ports are rare because the coast is buffeted by the south wind, rising from Africa. Nicaea touches the Alps, which, in turn, touch the cities of Deceatum and Antipolis. Thereafter is the Forum of Julius - Octavian's colony - and then: Athenopolis, Olbia, Glanum, Citharistes

& halycidon maſſilenſium portus: & in eo ipſa Maſſilia.
Hæc a phoceis oriunda:& olim inter aſperas poſita:nunc
ut pacatis ita diſſimillimis tamen uicina gentibus. Mirũ
q̃ facile & tunc ſedem alienam cœperit: & adhuc morem
ſuum teneat.Inter eam & Rhodanum maritima auatico-
rum ſtagno aſſidet foſſa mariana.Partem eius amnis nauigabilis alueo effundit.Alioquin littus ignobile eſt lapi
deum ut uocant:in quo Herculem contra albiona & bergion Neptunni liberos dimicantem cum tela defeciſſent
ab inuocato Ioue adiutum imbre lapidum ferunt. Credas
pluiſſe.Adeo multi paſſim & late iacent. Rhodanus non
longe ab Iſtri rhenique fontibus ſurgit.Deinde lemano la
cu acceptus tenet impetum:ſeq̃ per medium:integer agét
quantus uenit egreditur:& inde contra in occidentem ab
latus aliquandiu gallias dirimit.Poſt curſu in meridié ab-
ducto hac itrat:acceſſuque aliorum amnium iam grandis
& ſubinde grandior inter uolcas & cauaras emittitur. Vltra ſunt ſtagna Volcarum.Ledum flumen.caſtellum lata-
ra.me ſua collis incinctus mari pene undique:ac niſi q̃ an
guſto aggere continenti annectitur inſula.Tum ex gebé
nis demiſſus Arauraris iuxta Agatam. Secundum bliteras
orbis fluit. Atax ex pyreneo monte digreſſus:qua ui fontis
aquis uenit exiguus uaduſq̃.Eſt etiã ingentis alioquin al
uei tenens:niſi ubi narbonem attingit.nuſquã nauigabi-
lis.ſed cũ hibernis intumuit imbribus:unde eo ſolitus in-
ſurgere:ut ſe ipſe nõ capiat.Lacus accipit eũ Rubreſus nomine ſpatioſus admodũ:ſed q̃ mare admittit:tenuis aditu

and Halycidon, the Massilian port, and, in it, is Massilia itself. This place the Phoceans had first founded, having positioned it, in former times, among the uncivilized. But now - being entirely dissimilar - it has won over other nations to peace, and its habits are now accepted by others as a model of orderly ways. Yet it has retained its social customs. Between here and the Rhone, by the sea, is the Avaticorian lake and the canal near the ocean. The part of this which is navigable, is funded by the stream; the remainder is an ignoble bankside, known only for its boulders. It was here that Hercules fought against both Albionus and Bergion, the sons of Neptune; having used all his arrows, he invoked his father, Jove, who then rained down stones to give him aid. You may believe that it rained stones, for they lie about thick everywhere. The river Rhone rises not far from here, surging out of the fountains of the Ister and the Rhine. Then the stream carries into Lake Lemanus (Geneva) which contains its flow at the center, but, thereafter, it exits with the same force it entered. Turning, it moves to the west, and, with that, it divides Gaul for some length. Turning now to the south, and gathering other tributaries, it gains in magnitude and carries out between the Volscians and the Cavarians. Past here is the lake Volcarum, the river Ledum, the castle Latara and the hill Mesua - these are nearly cinctured about by the sea, and, except for a narrow land spit, they would be an island. Then, at Gebenna and Arauraris, it is divided near Agata, and is close to Blittera, on the river line. The flow of the Atax digresses from the Pyrenees heights, its stream bed running scant and shallow of itself, yet still a considerable flow, and, only where it touches Narbonne, is it navigable. Yet when it is increased by the waters of winter, it then surges so that its own bounds are not able to hold it. A lake accepts these waters - Lake Rubresus - a spacious body, but where it opens to the sea, the approach becomes attenuated.

Liber Secundus.

Vltra est Leucata littoris nomen: & salsule fons non dul/
cibus aquis deflues sed salsioribus & quā marinæ sunt:iux/
ta campus minuta arundine:gracilique peruiridis. Cæterū
stagno subeunte suspensus.Id manifestat media pars eius
quæ abscissa proximis uelut insula natat:pellicꝗ se atꝗ atra
hi patitur:quin & ex iis quæ ad imum perfossa sunt:suffu/
sum mare ostenditur. Vnde graiis nostrisque etiam aucto ꞏ
ribus:ueri ne ignorantia:an prudentibus etiam mendacii
libidine uisum est tradere posteris:in ea regione piscem e
terra penitus erui:ꝗ ubi ex alto hucusque penetrauit per ea
foramina ictu captantiū interfectus extraitur. Inde est ora
Sardonum:& parua flumina thelis & thicis:ubi accreuere
persæua.Colonia Ruscino.uicus eliberri magnæ quódam
urbis & magnarum opum tenue uestigium.Tum inter py
renei promontoria portus ueneris est sinu salso & ceruaria
locus finis galliæ.

Yreneus primo hinc in britānicum procurrit oc
ceanum:tum inter terras fronte cóuersus Hispa
niam irrūpit:& minore eius parte ad dexteram
exclusa trahit perpetua latera continuus per omnē donec
prouinciā longo limite immissus in ea littora:quæ occidē
ti sunt aduersa perueniat.Ipsa hispania:nisi qua gallias tā/
git:pelago undiꝗ incincta é:ubi illis adhæret maxime an
gusta paulatim se in nostrū & oceanum mare extendit:ma
gis magisꝗ latior ad occidentem abit: ac sit ibi latissima:
uiris:equis:ferro:plūbo:ære:argento auroꝗ & tam abun/
dans:& adeo fertilis:ut sicubi ob penuriā aquarū effœta &

Beyond here the shore line is called Leucata on account of a saline fountain which has no sweet water, but produces a stream higher in brine than the sea. Nearby is a small field made up of thin reed-like plants, ever having a rich green color. All around is a lake which enters below the field, and causes it to be suspended. This is made manifest at its central part where it is cut off from all that surrounds it, and the whole of it seems to float as an island, and is able to be drawn about as a bark shell. At whatever place its ground is cut away at the baseline, the sea itself may be observed. Afterward, the Greeks as well as our own authors - whether in ignorance or in mendacity toward the known truth - took the liberty of leaving behind, for posterity to read, that in this particular region the fish might be drawn up from the depths of the ground itself. Here it was, they claimed, that out of an opening in the ground anyone might catch and extract them. Thereafter comes the shore line Sardonum with its minor streams, the Thelis and the Thicis, which are given to sudden flooding. Next is the colony of Ruscino and the village of Eliberri, at one time a great city, but now it holds only a vestige of that wealth. Then, between the promontory of the Pyrenees and the port of Venus is the saline bay at Cerauria, and at this location is the border of Gaul.

The Pyrenees, at the outset, run toward the British Ocean: then, turning to the land front, they break across Spain. The minor part, to the right hand, extends in a continuous ridge, stretching at great length to the land's end by the sea, which determines the western limit. This, of itself, is Spain and is contingent to Gaul; otherwise it is cinctured about by the waters. At the place where it thus adheres, the landfall is constricted, not only by our own sea, but by the greater sea to its western side. Indeed, this is a place most plentiful - of men, horses, iron, lead, brass, silver, gold and this in abundance. But, perhaps in fertility, its figs and produce do suffer, to some extent, for a lack of water, and,

ſui diſſimilis eſt.Linum tamen aut ſpartū alat.Tribus au/
tem eſt diſtincta nominibus. Parſque eius Tarraconenſis:
pars Betica.pars Luſitania uocatur. Tarraconenſis altero
capite gallias.Altero beticam Luſitaniáq̃ contingens:ma
ri latera obiicit noſtro:qua meridiem: qua ſeptentrionem
ſpectat oceano.Illas fluuius anas ſeparat:& ideo betica ma
ria utraque proſpicit:ad occidentem atlanticum:ad meri/
diem noſtrum. Luſitania oceano tatūmodo obiecta eſt:
ſed latere ad ſeptentriones.fronte ad occaſum. Vrbium de
mediterraneis in terraconenſi clariſſimæ fuerunt Pallan/
tia & Numātia: nunc eſt Cæſarauguſta.in Luſitania.Eme
rita.in Betica:Aſtagi: iſpalis. Corduba. At ſi littora legas
a ceruaria proxima eſt rupes.Q uæ in altum pyreneū ex/
trudit.Deinthicis flumen ad Rhodam.Clodianū ad em/
poria. Tum mons Iouis cuius parti occidenti aduerſam
eminentiam cautium : quæ inter exigua ſpatia : ut gradu
ſubinde conſurgunt:ſcalas Hannibalis appellant.Inde ad
tarraconem parua ſunt oppida Blanda illuro: betullo:bar
chino.Subur.Tholobi:parua flumina Bettulo iuxta Iouis
montem Rubricatum in Barchinonis littore inter Subur
& Telobin maius taraco. Vrbs eſt in his oris maritima/
rum opulentiſſima Tulcis.Eam modicus amnis ſuper in/
gens Iberus deorſum attingit.Inde ſe in terras pelagus in/
ſinuat:& primum magno impetu admiſſum.mox in du
os ſinus promontorio:quod Ferrariam uocant:finditur
prior ſucronenſis dicitur: maiorque ac magno ſatis ore
pelagus accipiés: & quo magis penetratur:anguſtior So/

in this, it may be uncharacteristic to itself. Nonetheless, in linen flax and in matting it is well supplied. Three distinct names are here. Its one part is Tarraconensis, another is Boetica and the other is called Lusitania. Tarraconensis, at its one head, touches Gaul, and, with the other, Boetica and Lusitania. Its side projects to our sea on the south and, on the north, it overlooks the ocean. The river Anas separates them, and Boetica, beyond this point, looks over both seas. To the west is the Atlantic, and to the south is our sea. Lusitania, only by this manner, projects to the sea, but with its side toward the north and its front toward the west. Regarding the cities along the Mediterranean side: in Tarraconensis the finest had once been Pallantia and Numantia, but now it is Caesaraugusta (Saragossa). In Lusitania it is Emerita, and in Boetica there are Astagi, Hispalis and Cordova. But if the shore line here should then be read, it would show Ceruaria, and after would come a particular rock formation where the Pyrenees extrude outward. Thereafter is the river Thicis, running to Rhoda and the river Clodianus, running to Emporia. Then comes the mountain of Jove, whose western flank faces against a projection of stones so closely spaced together that the gradient sharply rises, and to this is applied the name, Hannibal's stairway. Following in the direction of Tarraconensis are small cities: Blanda, Illuro, Betullo, Barchino, Subur and Tholobi. The little stream, Bettulo, is near the mountain of Jove, with Rubricatum and Barchino on the shore between Subur and Tholobi. The finest city is Taraco, of all those that stand along this maritime way, and it is the wealthiest. The small river, Tulcis, courses above it, and below it runs the great Iberus. There the sea turns into the land, entering at the outset with great force, but later spreads into two bays at the location of the promontory called Ferraria. It is separated by the first, called Sucronensis, the larger of them. It has a large bay toward the sea, but at its greater penetration, it becomes constricted.

Liber Secundus.

robin & Duriam & Sucronem non magna excipit flumi/
na. Vrbes complexus & alias quidem:fed notissimas Va/
lentiam & Saguntum illam fide & ærumnis inclytam: fe
quens ilicitanus Alonem habeti & lucentiam:& unde ei
nomen est ilicen. Hic iam terræ magis in altum eunt:la
tioremcz q̃ fuerat. Hispaniam faciunt. Verem ab iis: quæ
dicta sunt:ad principia beticæ præter Carthaginem : quã
dux pœnorum Asdrubal condidit:nihil referendum est.
In illis oris ignobilia sunt oppida:& quorum mentio tan
tum ad ordinem pertinet. Virgi. in sinum quem Virgita
nũ uocant. Extra Abdera:suel:hexi:menoba. Malaca Sal
duba lacippo. Berbesul. Aperit deinde angustissimum pe/
lagus:& proxima inter se Europæ:atque aphricæ littora
montes efficiunt:ut initio diximus:colũnæ herculis abyla
& calpes:uterque. quidem sed calpes magis & pene totus
in mare prominens. Is mirum in modũ concauus. Ab ea
parte qua spectat occasum:mediũ fere latus aperit:atcz in/
de ingressus totus admodũ peruius prope quantũ patet si/
nus:& specus ultra est. In eocz Cartheia:ut quidam putant
aliquãdo tartessos:&. quã transuecti ex aphrica phœnices
habitant:atque unde nos sumus: cingent eratũ: mellaria:
& bello & besipho usqz ad iunonis promontoriũ orã freti
occupat. Illud iã in occidentē & oceanũ obliquo iugo ex/
currens atcz ei quod in aphricã ampelusiã esse dixeramus
aduersum:qua nostra maria sunt:finit Europen. Gades in
sula quæ egressis fretũ obuia est:admonet āte reliquas di/
cere:q̃ in oceani littora terrarũcz circuitum:ut initio pmi/

The Sorobis, the Duria and the Sucron do not constitute major tributaries. The notable cities around are Valentia and Saguntum; these are both held in renown for their long suffering. In sequence comes the bay, Ilicitanus, which has within it the cities Alone, Lucentia and Ilice, hence the name, Bay of Ilice. This, therefore, is the lie of the major land forms, and they make up the boundaries which comprise Spain. Indeed, from that which has been said, carrying even so far as to the borders of Boetica - it is, finally Carthage which ought to be noted. For the leader of the Poeni (the Phoenicians = the Carthaginians) was Hasdrubal, and it was he who built it. Yet nothing of it endures to the present day. Along the coast are several ignoble cities which should be mentioned merely for the sake of procedure. The town Virgi is within the bay called Virgita, and beyond are seen: Abdera, Suel, Hexi, Menoba, Malaca, Salduba, Lacippo and Berbesul. Following the narrows by the sea, on the coast between Europe and Africa, are the mountains we have spoken of earlier: the Pillars of Hercules - Abyla and Calpe (Gibraltar). Of these, Calpe is the greater in its thrust upon the sea. It is a marvel in its concave face, which fronts toward the west. At the middle of this flank it is nearly open in the manner of a bay, enough to permit passage, and terminates, then, into a cavern. In this place is Cartheia; some believe that, in times past, it had been Tartessos, the city where the Phoenicians traveled to from Africa, and then lived in it. This is the place that we are from. Mellaria, too, is cinctured around by the sea, as are the towns Bello and Besipho, which occupy the shore to the promontory of Jove. Running to the west, and at an oblique to the ocean, it would seem to join Africa with Ampelusia, just opposite to it, as we have spoken of. This, being at the place of our own sea, forms the boundary of Europe. The island of Gades (Cadiz) - as it is seen by those going outward through the narrows - admonishes me to speak of those remaining lands which are in a circuit about the ocean rim. Initially,

finus oratio excedat. Paucæ funt in mæotide.Inde enim
uidetur commodiffimum incipere:neque omnes tamen
incoluntur.Nam nec pabula quidem large ferunt.Hac re
habitantibus caro magnorũ pifcium fole ficcata:& in pul
uerem ufque contufa pro farre eft.Paucæ & in ponto.Leu
ce boryfthenis oftio obiecta parua admodũ:& q ibi Achil
les fitus eft:achillea cognomie.Non longe accollitur aria
quæ Marti facrata:ut fabulis traditur: tulit aues cum fum,
ma clade aduenientiũ pennas quafi tela iaculatas.Sex funt
inter iftri oftia.Ex iis.Pece notiffima & maxima. Thyn,
nias mariandynorum finibus proxima urbem habet:quã
quia bihtyni icolunt bithynida appellant. Contra thra,
cium bofphorum duæ paruæ: paruoque diftantes fpacio
& aliquando creditæ:dictæque concurrere:& cyaneæ uo,
cantur & fymplegades.In propontide tantum procone,
fos habitatur.Extra hellefpontum earum quæ afiaticis re,
gionibus adiacent:clariffimæ funt Tenedos figæis aduer
fa littoribus:& quo dicentur ordine ad promontorium
tauri montis expofitæ:quas quidam dici putauere Maca,
ron:fiue q fortunati admodum cœli folique funt: fiue q
eas fuo fuorumque regno Macar occupauerat:In Troade
lefbos:& in ea quinq olim oppida antiffa: Pyrrha. Eref,
fos.Ciraua.Mitylene.In ionia Chios & Samos. In Caria
cos.In Lycia Rhodos.In illis fingulæ funt iifdem nomi,
nibus urbes.In Rhodo tres quódam erant Lindos.Cami,
ros.Ielyfos:quæ contra Tauri promontorium importune
nauigãtibus obiacent Chelidoniæ nominant .In finu quẽ

I begin speaking of those beyond the shoreline. Few there are along Lake Maeotis -and, from that point, it would seem convenient to make our beginning. In addition, these are uninhabited because of their lack of adequate human sustenance. Those few who do live here, however, use the flesh of large fish dried in the sun, then pulverized, instead of farina meal. Only a few islands are found along Pontus. Leuce, at the bay of the Borysthenius, lies out only a small way, but it is still referred to as Achillea, that is, the place of his grave. Not far away are the dwellers of Aria, which is sacred to Mars. It is handed down by fable that it breeds birds which, from on high, cast feathers, just as deadly darts, upon all those entering. Six islands lie within the mouth of the Ister; of them, Peuce is the most noted and the largest. Thinnia, by the bay of Mariandyni, has a city founded by the Bithynians, and therefore called Bithynis. Just opposite to the Thracian Bosphorus are two lesser islands, spaced apart by only a small distance. At one time - if this should be credited - they were supposed to have been joined together, but called now, Cyaneae and Symplegades. In Propontus only Proconesus is inhabited. Beyond the Hellespont, with regard to those regions which are adjacent to Asia, the most renown is Tenedos by the shore of Sigaum, and, to speak of them in the order by which they are positioned from the promontory of Mount Taurus, are the isles of Macaron - whether called so by the turn of fortune or by the heavens, or whether because they had been once occupied by Macar, the king. Along the shore of Troy is the isle of Lesbos, having in past times, five cities: Antissa, Pyrrha, Eressos, Cirava and Mitylene. Along the shore of Ionia are the isles of Chios and Samos. Along the shore of Caria is the isle of Cos. Along the shore of Lycia is the isle of Rhodes, but within each isle is a single city of that same name. Yet on Rhodes, during former times, there were three cities, Lindos, Camiros and Ielysos. These, all being sited just opposite the promontory of Taurus, made navigation there inopportune, and so they are called the Chelidoniae. Within that bay, which

maximum Asia recipit prope media cypros ad ortum oc-
casumq; se immittens recto iugo inter ciliciam Syriasque
porrigitur ingens:ut quæ aliquando nomé regno cœperit
& nunc aliquot urbes ferat: quarum clarissimæ salamis &
paphos:& quo primum ex mari uenerem egressam accolæ affirmant: palæpaphos. Arados etiam in phœnice est
parua:& quantum patet tota oppidum frequens. tamen:
quia etiam super aliena tecta sedem ponere licet. Parua &
Canopos Nili ostio:quod canopicum uocant:obuia est.
Menelai gubernator Canobus ibi forte moriens nomen
insulæ:illa ostio dedit.Pharos Alexandriæ nunc pôte con
iungitur.Olim ut homerico carmine proditum é:ab eis-
dem oris cursu diei totius abducta:& si ita res fuit:uideri
potest coniectantibus in tantum mutatæ causas Nilū præ-
buisse:dum limum subinde:& præcipue cum exundaret:
littori adnectens auget terras spaciumque augescentium
in uicina uada promouet.In aphrica côtra maioré syrtim
cuteletos:contra minoris promontoria meninx:& cercin
na:contra earthaginis sinum Tarichiæ & ægates romana
clade memorabiles.Plures Europæ littoribus sunt appo-
sitæ.In ægeo mari prope thraciā Thasos.Imbros. Samo-
thrace.Scandille.polyægos. Scyathos. halonesos:& quã
aliquando omnibus qui mares erant:cæsis tantum fœminæ tenuisse dicuntur atho monti Lemnos aduersa.Paga-
seus sinus Scyathon prospicit.Scinison amplectitur. Eu-
bœa ad meridiem promontorium gereston & capharcā:
ad septentrionem caunum extrudit. & nusquā lata duum

is the greatest to be found in all Asia, lies the isle of Cyprus, located at about the midpoint. The isle runs nearly east to west, and contains a ridge in a line from Cilicia to Syria. At one time, it was the name of a kingdom, and now it possesses several cities. Of these the most famed are Salamis and Paphos. When first coming out of the sea, the goddess, Venus, had initially set foot (all of this affirmed by the local inhabitants) at Palaepaphos. The small isle of Arados is, in fact, Phoenicia, holding but a single city. It is well populated, however, because an alien is legally able to take up residence within any dwelling. Also small in size is the isle of Canopos at the mouth of the Nile, and the town is commonly referred to as Canopicum. Menelaus (according to Greek mythology) had, as the captain of his naval fleet, Canobus; and, by chance, he died on the island. Then, the entire mouth of the delta was given that name. The isle of Pharos and Alexandria are now joined by a bridge. In days of old, as is proved in Homer's song, it had been distanced by a whole day's travel from the mainland. It is, indeed, possible for this conjecture to be seen. Considering the vast changes caused by the force of the Nile - when its sands are carried forth and deposited - the shoreline itself is then augmented by the additional outward landshift. Along Africa, sited against the sandbank of the Greater Syrtis, is Cuteletos, and, sited against the promontory of the Lesser Syrtis, are Meninx and Cercinna. Sited against the bay of Carthage are Tarichiae and Agates; along here the great Roman defeat will be remembered. A great many more such isles are positioned along the shores of Europe. In the Aegean Sea, by Thrace, are found the isles: Thasos, Imbros, Samothrace, Scandille, Polyaegos, Scyathos, Halonesos and all of these, in former times, were so warlike (everyone so like Mars) that by nothing less than the cutting of heads, had the women been able to hold the power - so the matter is reported. At Lemnos, opposite Mount Athos, is the bay of Pagaseus, in view of Scyatho as well as Sciniso. This is south of the promontory of Gereston; Capharea is to the north of the projection of Caunum. Nowhere is its width more than a double

milium ſpacium habet ubi arctiſſima eſt. Cæterum longa
totique boetiæ appoſita anguſto freto diſtat a littore. Eu/
ripon uocant:rapidum mare & alterno curſu ſepties die:
ac ſepties nocte fluctibus inuicem uerſis: adeo immodice
fluens.ut uentos etiam ac plena uentis nauigia fruſtretur.
Aliquot in ea ſunt oppida heſtiæa eretria pyrrha neſos .
œchalia. Verum opulentiſſimæ caryſtos & chalcis. In atti/
de Helenæ eſt nota ſtupro helenæ & ſalamis excidio claſ/
ſis perſicæ notior circa peloponneſon etiã nunc in ægeo
phitiuſa & ægina epidaurico littori proxima. Troezenio
calauria inter ignobiles alias læto Demoſthenis nobilis.
In myrthoo cythera contra maleã emiſſa: & Teganuſa cõ
tra acritã. In Ionio ptehyria. Cephalonia. Neritos. Same.
Zacynthos. Dulychium:& inter nõ ignobiles Vlyſſis no/
mine Ithaca maxie illuſtris.In Eepiro Echinades: & olim
Plotæ nunc Strophades. Contra ambracium ſinũ Leuca/
dia:& uicina adriaco mari Corcyra. hæ thracum graiorũq̃
terris obiacent. At interius Melos.olearos.ægina. cothon
Ios.Therea.Gyaros. Hippuris. Dionyſſa. Cianos. Chal/
cis.Icaria.Pinaria.Niſyros.Lebyntohos.Calydnæ. Aſine
hæ qa diſperſæ ſunt Sporades.Ab eis Sicynus. Hipanos.
Sipanos.Seriphos.Henea.Paros.Syros. Tenos. Myco/
nos.Naxos.delos andros:qa in orbẽ iacẽt Cyclades dictæ
ſunt. Super eas iam in medio mari ingẽs & centũ quondã
urbibus habitataCrete ad orientẽ promontoriũ Samoniũ
ad occidẽtem criu metopon imittit:niſi maior eſſet: Cy/
pro ſimilis.multis famigerata fabulis.aduẽtuEuropæ:paſſ

mile across in its span, even at the place where it is the most constricted. The remainder
of it, however, is long, and its total length is positioned against Boetiae; both these being
separated by a narrow strait. Euripo this inlet is called; it bears a very rapid tide from the
sea, reversing itself no less than seven times a day and, again, seven times during the
night. So strong is the wind and current that all navigation is frustrated. A few towns are
located here: Hestiae, Eretria, Pyrrha, Nesos and Oechalia. In truth, the wealthiest are
Carystos and Chalcis. In Attica, not only is Helen well remembered, but also, the tragedy
of Helen. Salamis is remembered for the destruction of the Persian naval force. Around
the Peloponnese - yet still within the Aegean Sea - are the isles of Phitiusa and Aegina,
near the shore of Epidaurus. Troezene and Calauria are both counted among the obscure
ones, except for the last, which is elevated only through the fame of Demosthenes. In the
Myrtoan Sea are the isles of Cythera off Malea, and Teganusa off Acrita. In the Ionian
Sea are the isles of Protehyria, Cephalonia, Neritos, Samos, Zacynthos, Dulychium and,
by no means to be counted among the least, is the great name of Ulysses, who was from
Ithaca. Along the shore of Epiros are the Echinades Islands, together with the Plotae Isles,
called that name in times of old, but now known as the Strophades. Opposite to the bay
of Ambracium is Leucadia, and, in the vicinity of the Adriatic Sea, is Corcyra. Between
the Thracians and the Greeks are the isles located. But toward the center will be found
these isles: Melos, Oleros, Aegina, Cothon, Ios, Therea, Gyaros, Hippuris, Dionyssa,
Cianos, Chalcis, Icaria, Pinaria, Nisyros, Lebyntohos, Calydnae, and Asine. All of these,
however, being widely dispersed, are still the Sporades Islands. Passing beyond these are
the isles: Sicynus, Hipanos, Sipanos, Seriphos, Henea, Paros, Syros, Tenos, Myconos,
Naxos, Delos, and Andros. Lying nearly in a circle, they are the Cyclades. Past them,
in the sea, is that island where once a hundred cities stood - Crete - with the hills of
Samonium east and Metopon west. It is similar, if a bit larger, to Cyprus. Its fame
depends greatly on fables: the arrival of the goddess, Europa,

phaes & Ariadne amoribus. Minotauri feritate fatoque.
Dedali operibus & fuga. Tum ftatione atque morte:maxi
me tamen eo ꝙ ibi fepulti iouis pene clarum ueftigium fe
pulchrum:cui nomen eius infculptum effe accolæ often∕
dunt. Vrbium notiffimæ Gnoffos. Gortyna. Lyctos. Ly∕
caftos. Holopyxos.Ppœftos.cydon. Marathufa. dictina.
Inter colles ꝙ ibi nutritum Iouem accepimus : fama Idæi
montis excellit. Iuxta eft afticla. Naulachos zephyre. chrif
fe.gaudos:& quas mufagorus numero tres uno tamen uo
cabulo appellant:atque unde carpathio mari cognomen
eft carpathos. In adria abforos celadufe.abfyrtis. Iffa. Tru
cones. Hydria. electrides. nigra corcira: Tragurium. Dio∕
media. Aeftria:afine. atque ut Alexandriæ ita Brundufio
adiacens Pharos.

Icilia:ut ferunt aliquando cótinens:& agro bru∕
tio annexa.Poft freto maris ficuli abfciffa eft:Id
anguftum & anceps alterno curfu modo. in tuf∕
cum.Modo in Ioniū pelagus perfluit atrox. Sæuū & Scyl∕
læ Charybdifꝙ fæuis nominibus inclytum.Scylla faxū eft
Charybdis mare. Vtrūꝙ noxiū appulfis.Ipfa ingens & tri
bus pmótoriis in diuerfa pcurrés græcé litteræ imaginem
quæ delta dicit :efficit. Pachynū uocat :qd græciā fpectat.
Lilybeū qd in aphricā.Pelorū qd in italiā uergés fcyllæ ad
uerfum é caufa noís Pelorus gubernator ab Annibale ibi∕
dem códitus:qué idé uir pfugus ex africa ac p ea loca Syriā
petens:quia pcul intuenti uidebantur continua effe littora
& non peruium pelagus proditum fe arbitratus occide∕

the amorous tales of Pasiphae and Ariadne, the ferocity and the fate of the beast Minotaur, the works of the architect Daedalus and his final flight to the place of his entombment. But above all, is that location of the sepulchre of the god Jove, and this shows the clear trace of his name upon the sepulchre as being buried there - all of this the natives proudly show. The cities of note here are: Gnossos, Gortyna, Lyctos, Lycastos, Holopyxos, Phoestos, Cydon, Marathusa and Dictina. Among those hills where once Jove had accepted nourishment, stands the famed Mount Ida. Nearby are the hills: Asticla, Naulachos, Zephyre, Chrisse and Gaudos. The locale of Musagorus actually numbers three separate towns within itself, and these are called by that one name. Nearby, also, is found Carpathius, giving its name to the Carpathian Sea. Found in the Adriatic Sea are the isles: Absoros, Celaduse, Absyrtis, Issa, Trucones, Hydria, Electrides, Black Corcira, Tragurium, Diomedia, Aestria, Asine. Pharos isle is by Alexandria, and similar to Brundisium.

Sicily, so the tales are carried, was, at one time, contingent to the mainland, around the area of Bruttium. At a later time the sea cut into it, forming a strait, and, so, it carries an alternating current. It flows, on the one hand to the Tuscan Sea, and, on the other hand, to the Ionian Sea. Here the sea flow is atrocious, and it passes in a savage manner between the two famed points named Scylla and Charybdis. Scylla is a rock outcropping and Charybdis is a whirlpool of the ocean, both of them perilous to travellers. The island, of itself, is large and triangular in form, being divided by promontories so as to assume the image of a letter in the Greek alphabet known as Delta. Pachynus is the name of the first promontory which looks toward Greece; Lilybaeum is the second, which looks toward Africa; Peloris is the third, which looks toward Italy, at the verge of Scylla. This name was given to the place because Pelorus - buried here - was the captain of Hannibal's ship. Hannibal fled from Africa to seek asylum in Syria. From a distance, it appeared that the two shores joined together as one. Thus, Hannibal, thinking himself deceived, slew Pelorus there.

rat. Ab eo ad pachynum ora quæ extenditur Ionium mare attingens hæc fert illuſtria Meſſanam. Taurominium.
Catinam. Megarida. Syracuſas & in his mirabile arethu-
ſam . Fons eſt in quo uiſuntur iacta in alpheum amnē. ut
diximus peloponneſiaco littori infuſum. Vnde ille credi-
tur non ſe conſociare pelago: ſed ſubter maria terraſque
depreſſus huc agere alueum: atq̃ hic ſe rurſus extollere.
Inter pachynum & lilyæbum & agragas eſt: & heraclea &
therme. Inter lilybæum & pelorida panormus: & Imera.
Interius uero Leontini & centuripinum & bybla: aliæque
complures. Famam habet ob cereris templum ætna præ-
cipua montium. Erix maxime memoratur ob delubrum
Veneris ab Aenea conditum: & ætna quæ cyclopas olim
tulit: nunc aſſiduis ignibus flagrat. De amnibus Imera re-
ferendus: quia in media admodum ortus in diuerſa decur
rit: ſcindéſq̃ eam utrinq̃ alio ore in lybicum alio in tuſcū
mare deuenit. Circa Ciciliam in ſiculo freto eſt Aeæe: quā
Calypſo habitaſſe dicitur. Aphricā uerſus gaulos. Melita
coſura. Propius Italiam galata: Et illæ ſeptē: quas æoli ap
pellant oſteodes. Lipara. heratea. didyma. phœnicuſſa. eri
cuſſa. Aetna perpetuo flagrat igne. hiera & ſtrongylle &
pithecuſſa. Leucothea ænaria. Sidonia. capreæ. prochita.
Pontiæ. Pandatoria. Sinonia. Parmaria Italico lateri citra
tyberina hoſtia iacent. Vltra aliquot ſunt paruæ dianium
Iginiū. carbania. urgo. Ilua. caparia. Duæ grandes fretoque
diuiſæ ethruſco: quarum corſica littori propior inter latera tenuis & longa præterq̃ ubi aperta: & marianæ coloniæ

From there the shore extends to Pachynus, touching the Ionian Sea, and, along it, are the illustrious cities: Messina, Tauromenium, Catina, Megara, Syracuse and the wonderful fountain at Arethusa. It is the fountain in which may be seen those things which have been cast into the stream of the river Alpheus. This, as we have stated, issues into the sea off the Peloponnese. Here - if this point is to be credited - the flow does not conjoin with the ocean, but depresses itself below land and sea alike, only to reverse and carry outward again. Between Pachynum and Lilybaeum are found Agragas, Heraclea and Therme. Then, between Lilybaeum and Pelorida are Panormus and Himera. To the interior are the towns Leontini, Centuripinum and Bybla, among a number of others. Having a fame above all the rest is the temple found on Mount Aetna. Mount Erix is the most notable mountain because of its temple to Venus which was built by Aeneas. Aetna, in former times, had borne the monster Cyclops, but now, however, the mountain is ever ignited in flames. Of the rivers, the Imera must be referred to: it rises in the middle of the island, and diverts into contrary courses. The one falls toward the shore of Lybia, and the other devolves toward the Tuscan Sea. Around Sicily, in the Sicilian Narrows, is the isle of Aeaea, on which the princess Calypso is said to have lived. Africa, then, is directly opposite to the isles of Gaulos, Melita and Cosura. Near to Italy is the isle of Galata, along with the seven other volcanic isles which are known as the Aeolian Isles, namely: Osteodes, Lipari, Heratea, Didyma, Phoenicussa, Ericussa, Hiera. They burn with a perpetual fire just as Aetna - and also the isle of Strongylle. The isles of Pithecussa, Leucothea, Aenaria, Sidonia, Capri, Prochita, Pontia, Pandatoria, Sinonia and Parmaria all lie by the shore of Italy, along the near side of the Tiber's mouth. Along the far side, are the lesser isles of Dianium, Iginium, Carbania, Urgo, Ilua and Caparia. Two great islands divide the Tuscan Sea: of these, Corsica - closer to the mainland - is slender in length along the sides where it lies open at the sea, and both are maritime colonies. However,

Liber Tertius.

funt.A barbaris colitur Sardinia africū pelagus attingens:
nifi q in occidentē q in orientē anguſtius ſpectat: par &
quadrata undique & nuſquá non aliquanto ſpatioſior:q̄
ubi longiſſima eſt corſica.Cæterum fertilis & ſoli quá cœli
melioris:atq ut fœcunda ita pene peſtilés. In ea antiquiſ/
ſimi populorū ſunt.Ilienſes.Vrbium antiquiſſimæ Cala/
ris:& ſulci.At í gallia quas referre cóueniat ſolæ ſunt Stœ-
chades ab ora ligurū ad Maſſiliā uſq diſperſæ.Baleares in
hiſpania cótra tarraconéſia littora ſitæ non longe interſe
diſtát:& ex ſpatio ſui cognominibus acceptis maiores mi/
noreſq perhibent.Caſtella ſunt in minoribus Iamno &
Mago.in maioribus palma & polentia coloniæ. Ebuſos e
regione promontorii:qd in ſucronéſi ſinu Ferrariā uocát
eodē nomine urbem habet:frumétis tantū nó fœcūda :ad
alia largior: & oíum animaliū:quæ nocét: adeo expers:ut
nec ea quidé q̄ de agreſtibus mitia ſunt:aut generet:aut ſi
inuecta ſunt ſuſtineat.Cótra é colubraria cuius meminiſſe
ſuccurrit:q cū ſcateat multo ac malefico genere ſerpétū &
ſit:ideo inhabitabilis:tñ ígreſſis eā itra id ſpaciū: qd Ebu-
ſitana humo circūſignauerūt:ſine pernicie & tuta eſt iiſdé
illis ſerpétibus:q ſolét obuios appetere: aſpectū eius pul/
ueris aliudue qd̄ uerius pcur & cū pauore fugétibus.
Pōponii Melæ coſmographi. Liber tertius.

Icta eſt ora noſtri maris:dictæ iſulæ:quas am
plectitur : reſtat ille circuitus : quem ut initio
diximus:cingit oceanus ingens & infinitum

barbarians occupy the island of Sardinia, which touches the African Narrows. Except for being more narrow east to west, it resembles a square at the sides, but nowhere, along its length, is its volume very much greater than that of Corsica. The remainder of it is fertile, but the soil is better than the air rising above it; its richness actually becomes a pestilence. On it live a most ancient people, the Ilians. Their cities also are ancient, Calaris and Sulci. But along Gaul, however, the only thing convenient to make reference to are the Stoechades Isles, which are dispersed by the shore from Liguria to Massilia. The islands of the Baleares by Spain lie off the shore of Tarraconensis; they are sited at no great distance apart, and, according to their size (greater and less), they are known as Majorca and Minorca. The villages on Minorca are Iamno and Mago; on Majorca are the colonies of Palma and Polentia. At the Isle of Eubusus - by the bay of Sucronensis near the promontory of Ferraria - is a city of the same name, Sucron. It is not fruitful in the way of grain, but it is plentiful in other produce. Also, it is free from dangerous animals. These, having no part in so far as the domesticated animals are concerned, are able to breed only in the wild state. In contrast, is the adjacent isle of Columbraria (serpent). It breeds a multitude of poisonous snakes, and, thus, is inhabitable. However, if those entering here should carry with them some of the rich soil of Eubusus, they could proceed in safety. The snakes are ever ready to attack, but they can sense the presence of this dust. The creatures then turn in fear, and flee.

THE THIRD BOOK
Pomponius Mela, Cosmographer.

Our seacoast has been described, and its islands have been mentioned, as well as that which surrounds it. Yet, standing as in a circuit is that which we spoke of at the beginning - the Ocean - immense and infinite,

pelagus & magnis æstibus concitum: ita enim motus eius
appellant:modo inundat campos:modo late nudat ac re
fugit.Nunc alios aliofcz inuicem necz alternis accessibus:
nunc in hos:nunc in illos impetu uersum:sed ubi in om/
nia littora:quáuis diuersa sint terrarum insularumcz in me
dio pariter effusum est.Rursus ab illis colligitur.In medi/
um & insemetipsum redit.Tanta ui semper immissum:ut
uasta etiam flumina retroagat:& aut terrestria deprehen/
dat animalia:aut marina destituat.Necz adhuc satis cogni
tum est anhelitu ne suo id mundus efficiat:retractamcz cũ
spiritu regerat undam undicz:si ut doctioribus placet:unũ
animal é:an sint depressi aliqui specus:quo reciproca ma
ria residant:atque unde se rursus exuberantia attollant:an
luna causas tantis meatibus præbeat. Ad ortus certe eius
occasusque uariantur:necz eodem assidue tempore:sed ut
illa surgit ac demergitur:ita recedere atque aduentare com
perimus. Huc egressos sequentesque ea: quæ exeuntibus
dextra sunt:æquor atlanticum & ora bæticæ fontis excipit
quæ nisi cp semel iterumque paululum in semet abducitur
usque ad fluuium anam pene recta est. Turduli & bastuli
habitant.In proximo sinu portus est: quem gaditanum:
& lucus quem oleastrum appellant.Tum castellum Ebo/
ra in littore. & procul a littore asta colonia. Extra Iuno/
nis ara templumque est.In ipso mari monumentum Ge/
ryonis scopulo magis:cp insulæ impositum. Bætis ex ter/
raconensi regione demissus per hanc fere mediã diu:sicut
nascit :uno amne decurrit:post ubi nõ lõge a mari grãdẽ

that gathering of the great and surging swells, as its heavings are called. At first, they undulate into the fields, then turning again, they recede to leave them denuded. Now invaded by either one flow or the other, yet not one is identical to the other. Now drawing to itself, but now reversing with other swells along the coast lands and the islands, it at last flows into itself evenly, turning and gathering. So vast, always, in its force that it can even turn back the downstream current of the great rivers. In addition, it can apprehend the animals unaware by the shore, or it can leave the fish of the sea stranded on the land. Full knowledge does not exist whether its vast inhalation is caused by the world itself, or by the wind current issuing in every direction - as the learned doctors seem to accept - or if, as a living creature, it might depress itself within some cavern only to return as a reciprocal circuit when it reappears, or, instead, if the moon might be the actual cause of a movement so immense. For according to the phases of its rising and its setting, the sea certainly varies as well, not of its own accord, but with the rise and decline of the moon does it crest and fall. Those who voyage outward to follow along this shoreline, have, to the right hand, the unbounded surface of the Atlantic Ocean and the shorefront along the Baetica. Here is the stream of the river Anas, flowing sometimes in a small current, then sometimes withdrawing to itself, it resumes again the normal course. The Turdulians and the Bastulians inhabit this area. In near proximity is the bay of Gaditanum, and, along with it, a sacred grove of trees which is called Oleastrum. Then the village of Ebora is by the sea, but at some distance from the shore is the colony of Asta. Beyond here is the altar and the temple which is dedicated to Juno. In the sea itself is the monument of Geryon, sited upon a great outcrop of rock, somewhat similar to an island. The river Baetica, flowing from the region of Tarraconensis, cuts the area nearly at the midpoint, and the stream issues from a single spring at its headwaters. Past here, however, and not far from the sea, a great

Iacum facit:quaſi ex uno fonte geminus exoritur : quan
tuſque ſimplici alueo uenerat:tantus ſingulis effluit. Tum
ſinus alter uſque ad finem prouinciæ in flectitur: eumque
parua oppida olitingi. Oſſonoba cōtingunt. At luſitania
trans anam qua mare atlanticum ſpectat:primum ingen
ti impetu in altum abit. Deinde reſiſtit: ac ſe magis etiam
q̃ betica abducit.Q ua prominet bis in ſemet recepto ma
ri:tria prmontoria diſpergitur.Anæ proximum quia lata
ſede procurrens paulatim ſe ac ſua latera faſtigiat: cuneus
ager dicitur:ſequens ſacrum uocant.Magnum quod ulte
rius eſt.In Cuneo ſunt myrtilis balſa oſſonoba.In ſacro la
cobriga:& portus Annibalis.In magno ebora. Sinus in
ter ſunt:& eſt in proximo Salacia.In altero ulyſſipo.& ta
gi oſtium amnis aurū gemmaſque generantis. Ab iis pro
montoriis ad illam partem:quæ receſſit:ingens flexus ape
ritur.In eoque ſunt turduli ueteres:turdulorumq̃ oppida:
amnes autem in medium fere.Munda ultimi promonto
rii latus effluēs:& radices eiuſdem abluens Durius. frons
aliquandiu rectam ripam habet.Deinde modico flexu ac
cepto mox paulum eminet: tum reducta iterum iterum
que recta margine iacens ad promontorium:quod celti
cum uocamus:extenditur:totam celtici colunt:ſed a durio
adflexum groti.Fluuntque per eos Auo celandus.Næbis.
Minius & cui obliuionis cognomen eſt Limia.flexus ip
ſe Lambriacam urbem amplexus recipit fluuios. læros &
illam partem:quæ prominet:præſamarchi habitant:perq̃
eos Tamaris & Sars flumina non longe orta decurrunt.

lake is formed, as though rising from twin fountains, and flowing, however small, as one stream. Then, the bay once again deflects inward as far as the end of the province. Along the bay line, the small towns of Olitingi and Ossonoba are aligned. But in Lusitania, across the river Anas, the Atlantic Ocean may be seen, and here the land thrusts outward into the deep. From there it withdraws again, and recedes toward Boetica. At the place where it thrusts forward along two fronts, it receives the ocean, and here it is divided by three promontories. In proximity to the river Anas - following its broad side which gradually tapers off into a landspit - is the first which is known as Cuneus Field (The Wedge). The two promontories after this are known as Sacrum (The Consecrated) and Magnum (The Great). In Cuneus Field are found the villages of Myrtilis, Balsa and Ossonoba. In the Sacrum is the town of Lacobriga and the port of Hannibal. In the Magnum is the village of Ebora. Bays are spaced between these, and the nearest of them is Salacia. Then is the town of Ulyssipo and the bay of the river Tagus, from which gold and precious stones are extracted. From these promontories to that area which recesses, an immense bay opens far and wide. At this place are the ancient Turdulians, along with their cities. Nearly at the mid point is the river Munda, which flows by the side of the last promontory, and exactly at the base of it is the river Duria. This stream, for a considerable length, follows a straight course, then, after a slight deflection, flows in line again, but then, in another turning, follows in alignment by the promontory. This promontory we call the Celtic. The entire extent of this area is occupied by the Celts - from the river Durius to the bay of Gronium. Flowing through these parts are the rivers: Auo, Celandus, Naebis, Minius and that stream whose name represents oblivion, the river Limia. The bay itself holds the city of Lambriaca, along with the water course, the Laeros. In the projecting part of the bay, the Praemarchians are found; and in their area, are the rivers Tamaris and Sars; streams flowing not far from the shore.

Tamaris secundum Ebora pontum. Sars iuxta turrẽ Au
gusti titulo memorabilem. Cætera super Tamarici neriiq̃
incolunt in eo tractu ultimi. Hactenus enim ad occidentẽ
uersa littora pertinent: deinde ad septentriones toto late
re terra conuertitur. A celtico promontorio ad scithicum:
usq̃ perpetua eius ora: nisi ubi modici recessus ac parua p
montoria sunt. Ad cantabros pene recta est. In ea primũ
artabri sunt: & Ianasũm celticæ gentis. Deinde astures. In
artabros sinus ore angusto admixtum mare: non angusto
ambitu excipiens adrobicum urbem & quattuor amnium
ostia incingit. Duo etiam inter accollentis ignobilia sunt.
per alia duo meatus exit in libunca. In asturũ littore Noe
ga est oppidum: & tres aræ: quas sestianas uocant: in pe
ninsula sedent: & sunt augusti nomine sacræ: illustrantq̃
terras ante ignobiles. At ab eo flumine: quod saliam uocãt
incipiunt ore pulsati recedere: & latæ adhuc hispaniæ ma
gis magisq̃ spatia contrahere: usq̃ adeo semet & terras an
gustantibus: ut earum rerum spacium inter duo maria di
midio minus sit: qua Galliam tangunt: q̃ ubi ad occidentẽ
littus exporrigunt. Tractum Cantabri & uarduli tenent.
Cantabrorum aliquot populi amnesq̃ sunt: sed quorum
nomina nostro ore concipi nequeãt per eundem: & sa
lenos: saurium: Per autrigones & origemones quosdam
ne sua descendit: & deuil duplex triciũ tobolicum attingit
& deinde Iturissam & easonem: & magrada. Varduli una
gens hinc ad pyrenei iugi promontorium pertinens clau
dit hispanias. Sequitur galliæ latus alterum: cuius ora pri

The river Tamaris passes by Ebora, and then into the sea; the Sars passes by the renowned Turret of Augustus. The remainder of the area is occupied by the Tamaricans and by the Nerians, who are in possession to the end of the tract. To this point, these locations are aligned toward the western shore; from this point, however, the landmass turns toward the north. From the Celtic Promontory to Scythia the shoreline is continuous, except for those lesser bays and minor promontories. Toward the Cantabrians the line is nearly straight. Along here are the Artabrians and the Ianasians, both Celtic peoples. After them come the Asturians. Around Artabros the flow of the narrow bay inlet mingles with the sea, but the area is not narrow where it curves around the city of Adrobicum, which includes the four rivers encircling its bay. Two of these are insignificant, according to the local dwellers, but the other two, having a stronger flow, pass through the area of Libunca. Along the Asturian shore is the city of Noega, and three altars there which are called the Sestianae. They are sited on the peninsula, and they carry the sacred name of Augustus; the place may be illustrious now, but certainly was ignoble before. From here issues the river called the Salia, at the place where the shore begins to slightly recede. It is here that the breadth of Spain begins to contract, and its width between the seas begins to constrict. Here it is only half its breadth where it touches Gaul, running to the west. This tract is held by the Cantabrians and the Vardulians. Among the Cantabrians are various peoples and rivers - all having names which no Roman would attempt to pronounce. In this area are the streams Salenos and Sarium. Flowing through those tribes which are known as the Autrigones and the Origemones, the river Nesua passes. The river Devil branches through both Tricium and Tobolicum. Thereafter, through Iturissa, flow the streams Eason and Magrada. The Vardulians make up a single race from here to the Pyrenees, and with their extension to that promontory, they form the closure of Spain. Following in sequence, on the other side is Gaul, whose coast, at the outset,

mo nihil progressa in altum:mox tantumdem pene in pe
lagus excedens quantum retro hispania abscesserat: canta
brizis sit aduersa terris: & grādi circuitu afflexa ad occidē
tem littus aduersit. Tunc ad septentriones conuersa iterū
longo rectoque tractu ad ripas rheni amnis expanditur.
Terra est frumentī præcipue & pabuli ferax:& amoena lu
cis immanibus. Quicquid ex satis frigoris impaciens est
ager nec ubique alit:& noxio genere animalium minime
frequens. Gentes superbæ:superstitiosæ.aliquando etiam
immanes adeo:ut hominem optimam & gratissimam di
is uictimam crederent:manent uestigia ueritatis iam abo
litæ:atque ut ab ultimis cædibus temperant:ita nihilomi
nus ubi deuotas altaribus admouere delibant. Habent ta
men & facundiam suam:magistrosq; sapientiæ dryudas.
Hi terræ mundiq; magnitudinem & formam:motus cœ
li & syderū ac quid dii uelint:scire profitent.Docēt mul
ta nobilissimos gentis clam & diu nicenis annis in specu:
aut in abditis saltibus. Vnum ex iis quæ præcipiunt.i uul
gus effluit: uidelicet ut forent ad bella meliores æternas eē
animas uitamq; alteram ad manes.Itaq;cum mortuos cre
mant ac defodiunt:apta uiuentibus olim negociorum ra
tio etiam & exactio crediti deferbatur ad inferos: erātq;
qui se in rogos suorum uelut una uicturi libenter immit
terent. Regio quam incolunt omnis comata gallia. Popu
lorum tria summa noīa sunt:terminanturq; fluuiis ingen
tibus. Nā a pyreneo ad garūnam aqtania:ab eo ad sequa
nam celtæ. Inde ad rhenum pertinet Belgæ. Aquitanorū

does not project outward into the deep, but then, directly, it thrusts forward upon the sea nearly as much as Spain had receded. Cantabria here is the projecting land form, curving in a great circuit toward the west. But, in a long sweep, it advances to the north as far as the mouths of the river Rhine. The land is most productive in grain and fodder; amenable, rich and broad. Wherever a field might be found free from excessive cold, it can be cultivated, and would be fruitful; the more noxious types of wild animals are not frequent. The peoples are proud and superstitious. At one time they had been given to monstrosities, even to the belief that their gods were best gratified in human victims. There remains, yet, some vestige of this now outlawed practice. While, perhaps, they have been restrained from such extreme slayings, they still, however, do carry some to their altars of devotion in order to taste of their blood. Nonetheless, they indeed possess a certain eloquence, and their teachers are wise men known as Druids. With regard to the lands of the world, their magnitude and form, the motions of the heavens and the planets, the intentions of the gods - all these things they profess to know. Many things they teach, and to the most noble of their race they give secret instructions over a long period of time, even twenty years, in some cavern or in a concealed grove. One of their teachings is pre-eminent, and it has even flowed into the common store of human knowledge. It is this: that war and battle are for the better, since the immortality of the soul is preferable to the finality of the underworld. And when the dead are cremated and buried, it is appropriate to send along with them a rational account of their deeds when they were living to carry with them to the world beyond, so that they might ask for relief from any bond of debt. The region in which they live - taken as a whole -is called Comata Gaul. The population is generally known according to three names; these being determined according to three immense rivers. From the Pyrenees to the river Garunna is Aquitania, from the Sequana beyond here are the Celts. From there to the river Rhine are found the Belgians. Regarding the Aquitanians,

clariſſimi ſunt auſci Celtarum hedui. Belgarũ treueri. Vr/
beſque opulentiſſimæ in treueris auguſta. In heduis angu
ſtudunũ. In auſcis eluſaberrim. Garũna ex pyreneo mon/
te delapſus niſi cum hyberno imbre aut ſolutis niuibus in
tumuit: diu uadoſus: & uix nauigabilis fertur. At ubi obui/
us oceani exæſtuantis acceſſibus adauctus eſt: iiſdemqȝ re/
tro remeantibus ſuas illiuſqȝ aquas agit: aliquantum ple/
nior & quáto magis procedit: eo latior fit ad poſtremum
magni freti ſimilis nec maiora tantum nauigia tolerat: ue
rum ḗt more pelagi ſæuientis exurgens iactat nauigantes
atrociter utiqȝ: ſi alio uentus alio unda præcipitat. In eo eſt
inſula Antros nomine: quam pendere & attolli aquis in/
creſcentibus ideo incolæ exiſtimant: quia cũ uideatur edi/
tior aquis obiacet: ubi ſe fluctus impleuit illam operit: nec
ut prius tantum ambit: & qȝ ex quibus ante ripæ: colleſque
ne cernerentur obſtiterant: tunc uelut ex loco ſuperiore p/
ſpicua ſunt. A Garumnæ exitu latus illud incipit terræ p/
currentis in pelagus: & ora cantabricis aduerſa littoribus
aliis populis media eius habitantibus: ab ſantonis a doſiſ/
mos uſqȝ deflexa. Ab illis. n. iterum ad ſeptentriones frõs
littorum reſpicit: pertinentqȝ ad ultimos gallicarũ gentiũ
Morinos: nec portu: quḗ geſoriacũ uocant: quicquã habḗt
notius. Rhenus ab alpibus decidens prope a capite duos
lacus efficit uenetũ & acromum. Mox diu ſolidus: & cer/
to alueo lapſus haud procul a mari huc & illuc diſpergit .
Sed ad ſiniſtrũ amnis ḗt tum & donec effluat Rhenus ad
dexterá primo anguſtus & ſui ſimilis: poſt ripis longe ac

the foremost among them would be the Auscians; among the Celts it would be the
Heduans; among the Belgians it would be the Treverians. The wealthiest city among the
Treverians is Augusta; among the Heduans it is Angustodunum; among the Auscians it is
Elusaberrim. The river Garunna flows down from the peak of the Pyrenees. Except when
it might be imbued by the winter rain or by the melted snows, it flows for a great distance
by shallows, and it can hardly bear navigation. But when it approaches the ocean, it
increases the strength of its current, and augmented by its own volume, accepts additional
waters. Thus made more forceful, it runs broadly, in the semblance of a lake. Not only
is it able to carry navigation, but it has a strength as atrocious as the sea, with its motions
of wind and wave. At this point is the island named Antros. This isle seems able to both
rise and fall in accord with the waters of the tide - so the inhabitants suppose. It would
appear to be higher than the water lying around it, however, when the waves come to
cover the island, they seem only to flow about it, and the hills and the shore are seen then
as though viewed from some higher location. From this exit of the river Garunna, the
flank side of the landform begins its projection outward into the deep, and opposite to it
is the shore of Cantabria. Various tribes live around its center, beginning with the
Santones to the Osismians, on the side. From them, and turning once again to the north,
one may follow along the front of the shore as far as the ultimate border of Gaul, and to
the Morinian people. They do possess a port which is called Gesoriacum, but otherwise,
they have nothing worthy of note. The Rhine descends from the Alps, and near to its
headwaters, it forms two lakes, the Venetia and the Acromum. Thereafter, its flow runs
as a solid stream once more by a single channel, only to again divide not far from the sea,
and it is parted there. To the left side it is a river, until it surges outward - to the right side
the Rhine, at first, flows as a narrow channel within itself, but then its stream banks, at
length

Liber Tertius.

late recedétibus iã nõ amnis fed ingés lacus ubi cãpos im
plenit fleuo dicit eiufdéq nois infulã ãplexus fit iterum
actior:iterúq fluuius emittitur.

Ermania hinc ripis eius ufq ad alpes:a meridie
ipfis alpibus ab oriente farmaticarum confinio
gentium:qua feptétrione fpectat:oceanico litto
re obducta eft.Q ui habitant immanes funt animis atq
corporibus & ad infitã feritaté nafte utraq exercét: bellan
do animos:corpora ad cõfuetudines laborũ maxime fri／
gora nudi agũt:anteq puberes fint:& lógiffima apud eos
pueritia eft:uiri fagis uelantur aut libris arborum : quãuis
fæua hyeme nandi non patientia tantũ illis ftudium ét eft
bella cum finitimis gerunt:caufas eorum ex libidine accer
funt:neq imperitandi prolatandiq quæ poffident.Nam
ne illa quidem enixe colunt:fed ut circa ipfos quæ iacét ua
fta fint.Ius in uiribus habent adeo: ut ne latrocinii quidé
pudeat tantum hofpitibus boni:mitefque fupplicibus:ui／
ctu ita afperi incultiq ut cruda etiam carne uefcantur: aut
recenti aut cum rigentem in ipfis pecudum ferarumq co
riis manibus pedibufq fubigendo renouarunt.Terra ip／
fa multis impedita fluminibus. Multis montibus afpera:
& magna ex parte fyluis ac paludibus inuia. Paludũ Sue／
fia.Mefia & melfiagum maximæ. Syluarum hercynia &
aliquot funt:quæ nomen habet:fed illa dierum fexaginta
iter occupãs ut maior aliis:ita & notior.Montiũ altiffimi
Taunus & Rhetico:nifi quorũ noía uix é eloq ore roma／
no.Amniũ í alias gétes exeuntiũ Danubius & Rhodanus

recede widely to resemble not a river but a broad lake, which is able to invade the fields around. The flood here is called the Flevo, and it encircles an island of the same name; beyond here it falls, once again as a river, into the sea.

Germany, sited by this river, carries as far as the Alps, and its southern limits are the Alpine heights; to the east are the peoples of the Sarmatian tribes and to the north its boundaries overlook the Ocean. The inhabitants are giants, in both soul and body. By means of their inbred ferocity, and by their ceaseless wars, they are constituted, soul and body, to great labors, going naked in the cold, even throughout the long length of puberty. The men go about in blankets for cover, or in the bark of trees; even in the sharpest winter they take delight in swimming. Their occupation is war - perhaps with their near neighbors, perhaps with their close friends. This is not for reasons of domination, nor for any increase of possessions. For, indeed, it is not the urge to gain, but rather to lay waste to all that may be around them. The sole law that they have is that of force. Plunder is not thought of as wrongdoing, provided only that a kind of hospitality be shown to the needy and to beggars. Their victuals are bitter and uncouth; they feast on bloody meats, either taken directly from the slaying, or after a kneading by the hands and the feet into some degree of edibility. The terrain itself has the impediment of many rivers, as well as a number of difficult mountains, and, for the most part, it is impassable by reason of its forests and marshes. Of the marshes, the greatest are the Suesia, the Mesia and the Melsiagum. Of the forests, the greatest is the Hercynia; others may have the name, but this - the great forest - requires sixty days travel to cross. Of the mountains, the loftiest are the Taunus and the Rheticus; aside from some others which no Roman would attempt to pronounce. Among the rivers, considering only those which flow outward to other nations, are the Danube and the Rhone.

In Rhenum mœnis & lupia. In oceanum amiſius uiſurgis
& albis clariſſimi. Super albim codanus ingens ſinus magnis paruiſq; inſulis refertus eſt. Acre mare quod gremio
littorum accipitur: nuſquam late patet nec uſquam mari ſi
mile: uerum aquis paſſim interfluentibus: ac ſæpe tranſgreſ
ſis uagum atque diffuſum facie amnium ſpargitur. qua littora attingit ripis contentum inſularum non longe diſtan
tibus & ubique pene tantundem: ut anguſtum & par freto
curuanſque ſubinde ſe longo ſupercilio inflexum eſt. In eo
ſunt Cymbri & teutoni. ultra ultimi germaniæ hermiões.
Sarmatia intus quam ad mare latior ab iis quæ ſequuntur
Viſula amne diſcreta: qua retro abit uſque ad Iſtrum flumē
immittit. gens habitu armiſque particæ proxima. uerum ut
cœli aſperioris ita ingenii. non ſe urbibus tenent: & ne ſta
tis quidē ſedibus: ut inuitauere pabula. ut cædens & ſequés
hoſtis exigit: ita res opeſque ſecum trahens ſemper caſtra
habitat bellatrix. libera indomita. & uſque eo immanis atque atrox: ut fœminæ etiam cum uiris bella in eant: atq; ut
habiles ſint: natis ſtatim dextra aduritur mamma. Inde ex-
pedita in ictus manus: que exeritur. uirile ſit pectus. arcus tē
dere. equitare. uenari puellaria penſa ſunt. feriRe hoſtē adul
tarum ſtipendium eſt: adeo ut non percuſſiſſe pro flagitio
habeatur. ſitque eis pœnæ uirginitas. Inde aſiæ confinia ni
ſi ubi perpetuæ hyemes ſedent & intolerabilis rigor: ſcy-
thici populi incolunt fere omnes etiam in unum Sagæ ap
pellari. In aſiatico littore primi hyperborei ſuper aquilo-
né Ripheoſque montes ſub ipſo ſiderum cardine iacent:

Among those which flow into the Rhine, are the Moenis and the Lupia. Among those which flow into the Ocean, are the Amisius, the Visurgis and - the most noteworthy - the Albis. Terminating the river Albis is the great gulf of Codanus, which contains many islands, great and small. The saline ocean, when it runs along this shoreline, does not show itself at great length in the manner of a seashore, but rather it is intersected by other tributaries which penetrate outward to disperse themselves variously as watercourses. For this length the shore would seem to run partly as a lake and partly as an ocean bay. Along it are found the Cimbrians and the Teutons; beyond them is the ultimate border of Germany, and the Hermionian people. Sarmatia, wider at the center than at the sea, is framed by the rivers Vistula and Ister. Its dwellers, both in ways and arms, resemble Parthians. As the land is sharp and bitter, so, likewise, are the people. Without cities or fixed habitation, they move to new pastures, and according to hostile neighbors. All goods and possessions move with them. Free and indomitable, fierce and unrestrained - the women go to the battlefield along with the men. In order that they may grow accustomed to this, the right breast is burned away at the time of their birth that the right hand might become more adept with a weapon, and that they would tend to resemble men. To draw the longbow, to ride horseback, to hunt game, in all these things the maidens are trained. Thereafter, for them to have encountered the enemy in combat, is considered sufficient to warrant to them the stipend of manhood. But that no blow at all should be struck against the enemy, is considered the punishment for virginhood. Wherefore, to the confines to Asia they are sent, to its perpetual winter and its intolerable rigor. Here live the Scythian people, nearly all of them known by the single name, Sages. Along this Asiatic shoreline, first are the Hyperboreans, those people farthest north from Mount Rhipeus, and those located directly below the cardinal point of the polar star itself,

ubi fol non quotidie ut nobis: fed primum uerno æquino
ctio exortus auctunnali demum occidit. & ideo fex menfi
bus dies: & totidem aliis nos ufque continua eft. Terra an
gufta. aprica. per fe fertilis. cultores iuftiffimi. & diutiuf: quā
ulli mortaliū & beatius uiuūt: Q uippe fefto femper ocio
læti. non bella nouere. non iurgia. facris operati maxime
apollinis: quorum primitias delon mififfe initio per uirgi
nes fuas deinde per populos fubinde tradétes ulterioribus.
moremcʒ eum diu & donec uitio gentium téperatus eft:
feruaffe referuntur. habitant lucos fyluafcʒ. & ubi eos uiué
di fatietas magifcʒ tedium cepit: hilares redimiti fertis fe
metipfi in pelagus ex certa rupe præcipiti dant. Id eis funus
eximium eft. Mare cafpium ut angufto: ita longo etiam fre
to primum terras quafi fluuius irrumpit: atque ubi recto al
ueo influxit: in tres finus diffunditur contra os ipfum in
hyrcanum. ad finiftram in fcyticum. ad dexteram in eum
quem proprie & totius nominis cafpium appellant. omne
atrox fæuum. fine portibus: procellis undique expofitum
ac belluis magis quam cætera refertum: & ideo minus naui
gabile. ad introeuntium dextram Scythæ nomades freti
littoribus infident. Intus funt ad cafpium finum cafpii et
amazones: fed quas fauromatidas appellant. ad hyrcanum
Albani & mofchi: & hyrcani: In fcythico Amardi & pfici.
etiam ad fretum debrices. Multi in eo finu magni paruicʒ
amnes fluunt: fed qui famam habent ex ceraunis mótibus
uno alueo defcendit duobus exit in cafpium araxes tauri
latere demiffus. quod cāpos armenie fecat: labit placidus

where the sun does not rise and set daily as we know it, but at the beginning of the spring equinox it quickly rises, and does not set again until the autumnal equinox. Therefore, there are six months of daylight, and six months of continual night. The land is limited, but where it is exposed to the sun it can be cultivated; the dwellers are entirely honest, long lived and enjoy a blessed existence. They always delight in a happy gathering, they know nothing of war or litigation, and, in regard to sacred matters, their god is Apollo. In regard to their first fruits, they had, at one time, been taken to the island of Delos by their own virgins, but later they were sent through other nations around them, each tribe passing onward to the next. This custom existed for a long while, until it was discontinued by the other nations. They inhabit the woodlands and the forests. When, at last, they have lived long enough and their existence becomes tedious, they adorn themselves in garlands and, with a sense of hilarity, they cast themselves from a certain rock into the sea. This is their most esteemed funeral custom. The Caspian Sea, on a narrow front, first enters the landmass as a lengthy body of water not unlike the inrush of a river and, at last, its course diverges into three bays. First, (opposite to the mouth of the sea) is the bay of Hyrcanum, second, (to the left hand) is the bay of Scythia and third, (to the right hand) is the bay known as the Caspian bay proper. All of these waterways are atrocious and fierce - all without ports and stormswept, everywhere exposed to all the elements, as well as to wild beasts. Therefore, it is unnavigable. At the right, upon entering this sea, are the Scythian nomads along the shore. In the Caspian Bay, are the Caspians and the Amazons, both known as the Sarmatians. In the Hyrcanum Bay, are the Albanians, the Moschians and the Hyrcanians. In the Scythian Bay, are the Amardians, the Persians and, at the entrance, the Debricians. Rivers, both great and small, flow to the shore. The most famous courses from Mount Ceraunis as a single stream, but enters the Caspian Sea in two channels. The River Araxes issues from the side of Mount Taurus. Flowing through the plains of Armenia, its movement there is placid,

& filens:neꝗ in utram partem eat:q̄q̄ intuearis: manif e
ſtus cū in aſperiora deuenit hinc atꝗ illinc rupibus preſſus
& quanto anguſtior:tanto magis pernix. frangit ſe ſubin
de ad oppoſita cautium atꝗ ob id ingenti cū murmure ſo
nanſꝗ deuoluitur adeo citus : ut qua ex præcipiti caſurus
eſt:in ſubiecta non declinet ſtatim undam: ſed ultra q̄ ca
nalem habet:euehat plus iugeris ſpatio ſublimis : & aquis
pendentibus ſemetipſum ſine alueo ferens. deinde ubi in
curuus arcuatoꝗ amne deſcendit:ſit tranquillus iterumꝗ
per campos tacitus & uix fluens. In id littus elabitur cyrus
& cambyſes ex radicibus coraxici mōtis uicinis editi: & in
diuerſa abeunt. perꝗ hiberas & hyrcanos diu & multum
diſtantibus alueis defluunt. poſt non longe a mari eodem
lacu accepti in hyrcanum ſinum uno ore perueniunt. Ia
xartes & oxos per deſerta ſcythiæ ex ſogdianorum regio
nibus in ſcythicum exeunt. ille ſuo fonte grādis. hic incur
ſu aliorum grandior:& aliquandiu ad occaſum ab oriente
occurrens iuxta Dahas primum inflectitur : curſuꝗ ad ſe
ptentrionem conuerſo inter amardos & peſicas os aperi
tur. Syluæ alia quoꝗ dira animalia uerum & tigres ferunt
utiꝗ hyrcaniæ ſæuum ferarum genus:& uſꝗ eo pernix: ut
illis longe quoꝗ progreſſum equitem conſequi:nec tan
tum ſemel:ſed aliquotiens etiā:curſu unde cœperit:ſubin
de repetito:ſolitū &facile ſit. Cauſa ex eo eſt:ꝗ ubi ille in
terceptos earum catulos citus cœpit auehere: & rabiem ap
propinquantium fruſtraturus: aſtu unū de pluribus omit
tit. hæ piectū accipiūt: & ad cubilia ſua referūt:rurſumꝗ &

and quiet as a lake, even to the point where the direction of its current cannot be determined. But beyond this area it flows through a rock-lined narrows, and the more constricted it becomes, the faster the current. The movement is broken up by the stones of the streambed, and the result is a violent onrush with a great volume of sound. So great is the cascade that it would seem to devolve itself almost above and free from the river course proper - carrying on in this manner for nearly the length of a field, only to return, once again, as a tranquil and gently rolling watercourse, as before. It is from this shore, from the base of Mount Coraxis, that the rivers Cyrus and Cambyses set out by two diverse ways, travelling far and at great length through the lands of Hiberas and Hyrcania. The two ways finally merge, as one, near the sea, to form a lagoon at Hyrcanum bay. Here are found the rivers Iaxartes and Oxos, as they pass out of the Scythian Desert from the region of the Sogdianians, and the two empty into the Scythian Bay. The first has a strong flow from its initial fountainhead; the second is made strong by the incursion of its tributaries. The direction of flow, in general, is from east to west, and the course enters into the area of the Dohanians, then, curving northward, passes between the Amardians and the Persians. In the forests of this land live many dire animals, but, above all, it is the dwelling place of the dreaded Hyrcanian tigers. So fierce and so swift are these frightful creatures that they are able to pursue and overtake riders mounted on fleet horses. They are seen to do this not only once, but to return from their lairs, and pursue others as well. This is caused by the action of the horsemen, who, having captured a number of the young cubs, begin their rapid escape. Then, in order to avoid the fury of the pursuing tiger, the horsemen cast down a single whelp. This cub is carried back, at once, to the lair. But the tiger, when it returns,

sæpius remaneant atqz idé efficiunt:donec ad frequétiora
q̃ adire audeant: pfugus raptor euadat.Vltra caſpiũ ſinum
quidnã eſſet: ambiguum aliquandiu fuit. Idé ne oceanus
an tellus in ſeſta frigoribus ſine ambitu:ac ſine fine piecta:
Sed præter phyſicos Homerumqz:q̃ uniuerſum orbé ma
ri circumfuſum eſſe dixerunt.Cornelius nepos:ut recentior
auctoritate:ſic certior.teſtem autem rei.Q u. Metellũ ce
lerem adiicit:eumqz ita rettuliſſe commemorat. Cum gal
liis proconſul præeſſet.Indos quoſdam a rege Sueuorum
dono ſibi datos.Vnde in eas terras deueniſſent reqrendo
cognoſſe ui tempeſtatum ex indicis æquoribus abreptos
emenſoſqz:quæ intererant:tandem in germaniæ littora
exiiſſe.Reſtat ergo pelagus.Sed reliqua lateris eiuſdem aſ
ſiduo gelu durantur.& ideo deſerta ſunt. His horis quas
angulo beticæ adhucuſqz perſtrinximus multæ ignobiles
inſulæ & ſine nominibus etiã adiacét:ſed earum:quas p̃te
rire non libeat:gades fretum attingit:eaque a continenti
anguſto ſpatio & ueluti flumine abſciſſa:qua terris ppior
eſt pene rectam ripam agit.Q ua oceanum ſpectat duo
bus promontoriis euecta in altum mediũ littus abducit:&
fert in altero cornu eiuſdem nominis urbem opulentam.
In altero templum ægyptii Herculis conditoribus religio
ne:uetuſtate opibus illuſtre.Tyrii condidere:cur ſanctum
ſit:oſſa eius ibi ſita efficiunt.Annorum quis'manet ab ilia
ca tépeſtate principia ſunt.Opes tépus aluit.In Luſitania
erythia:quã geryone habitatã accepimus:alieqz ſine certis
nominibus adeo agri ſertiles:ut cũ ſemel ſata frumta ſint,

however, the chase is once again resumed until the horsemen finally reach a place where the tiger chooses not to enter, and so the thief escapes. Whatever lies beyond the Caspian boundaries has remained, for a long time, completely ambiguous. Some have supposed it to be either the Ocean or a great landmass, infected by the cold, and extending on and on without known borders. Before the time of the natural philosophers and Homer, the whole of the universal orbit was said to be cinctured around by the sea. Cornelius Nepos, a recent author and a credible authority, has addressed this matter. He has cited Quintus Metellus - sometimes referred to as "The Swift One" - by quoting a report he once submitted when he had been the proconsul of Gaul. He reported that one time he had been given several Indians as a gift from the king of the Sueian people. When Metellus asked them how they had first arrived in that land, he was told that a tempest had driven them away from the seas off India, and, being shipwrecked, they had wandered, unknowingly, as far as the area of Germany. This would seem to establish the presence of an encircling ocean, but its entire shoreline, however, is afflicted by the extreme cold, and it remains always uninhabited. Nonetheless, from all the shorelines which have been spoken of before - even from the limits of Boetica to here - small islands are strewn about, many of them nameless. Of those which have not yet been discussed, the isle of Gades lies within the narrow outlet, a strait between itself and the land, hardly a sea lane apart; the two shores are nearly in contact. On the ocean side of the island, are two promontories facing the deep. In the cleft between, is the rich city of Gades. On the opposite side, is the Egyptian temple of Hercules, built by his followers. It is ancient and famous, first erected by the people of Tyre. It is held sacred on his account; his bones are buried within. The years that have passed, since that time, have grown into ages, and all the centuries have magnified its wealth. By Lusitania, is the isle of Erythia, where the giant Geryon lived, so we are told. Other islands lie about without names, yet with fertile fields. So rich is their grain

ſubinde recidiuis. ſeminibus ſegetē nouantibus ſeptē mi-
nimū interim plures etiā meſſes ferant. In celticis aliquo
ſunt: quas quia plūbo abundant. uno omnes nomine caſ-
ſiterides appellant. Sena in britannico mari oſiſmicis aduerſa littoribus gallici numinis oraculo inſignis eſt: cuius antiſtites perpetua uirginitate ſanctæ numero nouem
eſſe traduntur. Galſicenas uocant: putantqʒ ingeniis ſingu
laribus ꝑditas: maria ac uentos concitare carminibus. Seqʒ
in quæ uelint animalia uertere: ſanare: quæ apud alios in
ſanabilia ſunt. Scire uentura. & ꝑdicare: ſed nō niſi dedita
nauigātibus: & in id tantū: ut ſe cōſuleret profectis.

  Ritānia qualis ſit: qualeſqʒ pro generet: mox cer-
  b tiora & magis explorata dicent. Q uippe tā diu
  clauſam aperit ecce principū maximus nec indo-
mitarū modo ante ſe: uerū ignotarū quoqʒ gentiū uictor:
propriarū rerū fidem ut bello affectauit ita triumpho de-
claraturus portat. Cæterū ut adhuc habuimus: inter ſepten
trionem occidentemqʒ proiecta grandi āgulo rehni oſtia
proſpicit. Deīde obliqua retro latera abſtrahit. Altero gal
liam: altero germaniā ſpectans. Tum rurſus perpetua mar
gine directi littoris ab tergore abducta: iterum ſe in diuer
ſos angulos cuneat triquetra: & Siciliæ maxime ſimilis:
plana. ingens: fœcunda: uerum iis quæ pecora. q̃ homines
benignius alant. Fert nemora: ſaltus ac prægrandia flumina alternis motibus modo in pelagus: modo retro fluen-
tia: & quædam gēmas margaritaſque generantia. Fert po
pulos regeſqʒ populorum: ſed ſunt inculti omnes atque ut

that as the seed grain is sown in the cornlands, no less than a seven-fold crop, or more, may be gathered. Along the Celtic shoreline are found other islands having abundant deposits of lead, and all of them are referred to under the single name of the Cassiterides Islands. The isle of Sena, in the British Ocean, is opposite to the shoreline of the Osismians, and it is famed for its Gallic oracle. Its priestly class is made up of perpetual virgins; the numeral nine being held sacred among them. They are called the Gallicenes, and they are thought to possess a singular wisdom. The waters and the winds are summoned by means of their singing. Thereafter, they are able to change themselves into whatever animal they may choose. They can heal those whom others are not able to heal. They know of the future, and predict events, but only to those travellers who seek advice for their affairs.

Britain - with regard to its nature and the people who live there - we shall soon be able to speak with greater asssurance. It has long remained an uncertain area, yet, lo, our own great Commander-in-Chief is about to set out, as a victor, to that unknown land. Then, when he shall return in triumph, carrying the spoils of war, he shall bring us a full account. Nonetheless, certain aspects of the place we do presently know. Toward the north and west, it projects broadly away from the outlet of the Rhine waterway. From there, its one side draws back at an oblique, the second side fronts Gaul, and the third side overlooks Germany. Its far shoreline follows the coast and it becomes triangular in form. Where it is an open plain, it somewhat resembles Sicily; its soil is fertile, but more favorable to herds than to the population. It bears large wooded areas and great rivers, and the tides are hardly less than those of the sea. In the tidal lands, gems and pearls are sometimes found. It possesses noble kings and noble tribes. Yet, they are entirely uncultured, and

longius a continenti abſunt:ita aliarum opum ignari ma⸗
gis.Tantū pecore ac finibus dites.Incertū ob decorem:an
quid aliud ultro corpora infecti:Cauſas autē & bella con⸗
trahunt:ac ſic frequenter inuicem infeſtant:maxime impe
ritandi cupidine ſtudioque ea prolatandi: quæ poſſident.
Dimicant non equitatu modo aut pedite:uerū & bigis &
curribus gallice armati. Couinos uocant: quorum falcatis
axibus utuntur.Super britanniā Iuuerna eſt:pene par ſpa⸗
cio. Sed utrincǫ æqualis : tractu littorum oblonga.Cœli
ad maturanda ſemina iniqui.Verum adeo luxurioſa her⸗
bis non lætis modo.ſed etiam dulcibus:ut ſe exigua par⸗
te diei pecora impleant:& niſi pabulo prohibeantur:diu⸗
tius paſta diſſiliant. Cultores eius inconditi ſunt & oīum
uirtutum ignari quā aliæ gentes:aliquatenus tamen gnari.
pietatis admodum expertes.Triginta ſunt orchades angu
ſtis inter ſe diductæ ſpatiis. Septem hemodes contra ger⸗
maniam uectæ in illo ſinu:quem codanū diximus. Ex iis
Codanonia:quā adhuc Teutoni tenent & ut fœcunditate
alias:ita magnitudine ante ſtat. Q uæ Sarmatis aduerſa
ſunt ob alternos acceſſus recurſuſque pelagi & quot ſpacia
quis diſtant: modo operiuntur undis: modo nuda ſunt.
Alias inſulæ uidentur: alias una & continens terra .In his
eſſe oonas:qui ouis anium paluſtrium: & auenis tantum
alantur:eſſe equinis pedibus hippopodas:& Satmalos q⸗
bus magnæ aures & ad ambiendum corpus omne patulæ:
nudis alioquin prouecti ſunt præterquā quod fabulis tra⸗
ditur auctores etiā quos ſequi non pigeat: inuenio. Thule

the farther they are from the continent, and away from its riches, the more ignorant they are. But they are well supplied, however, in herd animals and in ample grazing lands. It is uncertain whether for reasons of decoration, or for some other purpose, they dye their entire bodies. They generate causes for war, frequently against one another, and usually based on the desire for command and the desire for greater possessions. They battle not only on horseback and foot, but also on wagons and chariots - using Gallic armaments. The chariots are called covini, and they employ scythes attached to the axles. Beyond Britannia is Hibernia, very nearly its equal in volume. Although the sides are generally similar, its shoreline retracts to form an oblong shape. Its atmosphere would seem to be ripe enough, yet the place is not well suited for seed grain. Certainly, however, the native vegetation is luxurious and sweet; so rich, in fact, that should the flock animals be permitted to graze without restraint, they would become bloated on the rank grass. The inhabitants here are uncouth and with no redeeming virtue - to an extent greater than observed in any other nation. Whatever virtue might exist with them, it would have little to do with culture. Thirty islands lie offshore, closely spaced, and known, together, as the Orchades. Seven other islands - the Hemodes - are sited at an angle toward the waters off Germany, in the gulf which we call the Codanus. Codanonia is the shoreline there, and is held by the Teutons; the area is large and fruitful. Other isles, those lying off Sarmatia, are in the ebb and flow of the channel tides, and are sometimes submerged and sometimes dry land. When first viewed, they appear to be part of the mainland. Here live the Oenian people, subsisting solely on the eggs of shore birds, which they cook into a paste. There, also, are seen the Hippopodian people, whose feet would seem to resemble the hooves of horses. Here, also, are the Satmalians, whose extraordinary ears appear to enclose their entire bodies, which are otherwise naked. The aforementioned cases could be fabulous, but they are supported by authors known to be trustworthy. Thule

belgarũ littori appofita eft graiis & noftris celebrata carmi
nibus. In ea cp fol longe occafurus exurgit breues aticp no∕
ctes funt: fed per hyemé ficut alibi obfcuræ æftate lucidæ:
cp per id tépus iam fe altius euehens q̃q̃ ipfe non cernatur
uicino tamen fplendore proxime illuftrat: per folftitiũ ue
ro nullæ: cp tum iam manifeftior non fulgore modo: fed
fui quoque partem maximam oftétat. Talge in cafpio ma
ri fine cultu fertilis: omni fruge ac fructibus abundãs. Sed
uicini populi quæ gignuntur attingere nefas: & pro facrile
gio habent: diis parata exiftimantes: diifque feruanda. Ali
quot & illis oris: quas defertas diximus æque deferte adia
cent: quas fine propriis nominibus fcythicas uocãt. Ab iis
in eorum recurfus inflectitur: inque oram terræ fpectantis
orientem pertinet. Hæc a fcythico promontorio appofi∕
ta primũ ois quæ eft in uia: deinde ob immanitatem habi
tantium inculta∙Scythæ funt androphagæ & ∙Sagæ diftin
cti regione: quia feris fcatet: in habitabili: uafta deinde ite
rum loca belluæ infeftat: ufcp ad montem mari iminenté
nomine thabim. Longe ab eo Taurus attollitur. Seres in∕
terfunt genus plenũ iufticiæ & cõmercio: cp rebus in folitu
dine relictis abfens peragit.

Otiffima India non eoo tantũ appofita pelago
fed & ei quod ad meridié fpectãs idicũ diximus
& hinc tauri iugis: ab occidéte inde finita: tantũ
fparium littoris occupat quantum per fexaginta dies no∕
ctefcp uelificantibus curfus eft. Ita multũ a noftris abducta
regionibus: ut in aliqua parte eius neuter feptentrio appa

is the isle sited opposite to the Belgian shoreline. The islanders are famed for their chanting in Greek songs and in our own hymns. Here, the rising and setting of the sun are so distant that night is foreshortened. But the winter is as dark as the summer is light. The south light becomes obscure, and it radiates only a lucidity that seems a reflection. During the summer solstice, there appears to be no real night; the sun crests to a refulgence in its high orbit. The isle of Talge, in the Caspian Sea, has few plowed lands, yet it is bears crops and fruit. The natives think that nothing growing should be touched, but reserved for the gods. We speak of the desert shore and the desert isles, either unnamed or called the Scythian Islands. The curving shore here turns eastward. The Scythian Promontory is opposite the first landfall, which contains no roadway. Beyond here the tribes are wild. The Anthropophagae and the Sagae are both Scythian, but occupy different regions. The farthest removed inhabit a great desert, a place for wild beasts which extends as far as the Thabim Mountain Range. Mount Taurus is a great distance away, and the Seres tribes inhabit the land lying between. They are an honest people, and in their commercial trade, they place goods in a safe cache, and go on their way.

Noteworthy, indeed, is the land of India, opposite not only the sea, but also opposite to the sea of the South, which we have spoken of as the Indian Ocean. From there, it is bounded on the west by Mount Taurus. So great is the length of its shoreline that a voyage of not less than sixty days and nights of travel, under full sail, are needed to pass it. Far removed from us are some of these regions, and neither side of its northern part is readily apparent,

Liber Tertius.

reat:aliterq; quã in aliis oris umbræ rerũ ad meridiẽ iacẽt:
Cæterũ fertilis:& uario genere hominũm aliorũq; anima
lium scatet. Alit formicas non min us maximas canibus:
quas more gryphorum aurũ penitus egestum cũ summa
pernicie attingentium custodire cõmemorant. Immanes
& serpentes aliqui:ut elephantes morsu atque ambitu cor
poris afficiãt tã pinguis alicubi &tã feracis soli:ut in eã ella
frondibus defluãt.Lanas syluæ ferãt.Arũdinũ fissa iterno
dia ueluti nauitas binos & q̃dã ternos ẽt uehant. Cultorũ
habitus moresq; dissimiles. Lino alii uestiuntur aut lanis
quas diximus.Alii ferarũ auiũq; pellibus:pars nudi agunt:
pars tantũ obscena uelati.Alii humiles paruiq;:alii ita p
ceri & corpore ingẽtes: ut elephantis etiam & ibi maxi
mis sicui nos equis: facile atq; abiliter utantur. Q uidam
nullũ animal occidere.nulla carne uesci optimũ existimãt
Q uosdã tantũ pisces alunt.Q uidam proximi parentes
priusquã annis aut ægritudine in maciem eant:uelut ho
stias cædunt cæsorũq; uisceribus epulari fas &maxime piũ
est.At ubi senectus aut morbus incessit: procul a cæteris
abeunt mortéque in solitudine nihil anxii expectãt. Pru
dentiores:eis quibus ars studium sapientiæ contingit: nõ
expectant eam : sed ingerendo semet ignibus læti & cũ
gloria arcessunt.Vrbium quas incolunt sunt autem plu
rimæ.Nisa est clarissima & maxima.Montiũ Meros Io
ui sacer.Famam hinc præcipuam habent.In illa genitum.
In huius specu liberũ arbitrant ̃ eẽ nutritũ:unde græcis au
ctoribus: ut femori Iouis isutũ dicerẽt:aut materia inges

except that at its extreme limit the shadows are known to fall to the south. All the remainder of it, however, is fertile and possesses various types of men and animals. The country breeds ants which develop to the size of grown dogs. These insects resemble the griffins, and are able to extract gold out of the earth, and the gravest dangers would befall all those who attempt to lay hands on it. In addition, there are serpents so immense that even the elephants can fall prey to their biting and their coiling. In certain areas the soil is so enriched that honey falls off the foliage of the trees. Some of the trees also carry linen flax. With regard to certain cane reeds, should they be split in two, they are able to be formed into skiff-like boats, capable of floating two men, or possibly three. The inhabitants, in both dress and custom, are dissimilar. Some are vested in flax, and others are dressed in the linen we have spoken of; others go about in skins and the feathers of birds, while some go naked or covered just enough to check obscenity. Some of the men are short and small, but others are so huge in body that they can mount and ride an elephant with the same facility that we might ride a horse. Certain ones among them would never slay an animal, nor would they think of eating meat. Certain others live solely on fish. Some of them slay their own parents and near relations before they reach the time of decline and old age; they suppose that by dissecting the corpse and feasting on the viscera, is to offer up the maximum act of piety. But when old age does appear, those so afflicted depart from society, take themselves to a solitary place, and, without any show of anxiety, they wait for death. The philosophers among them, however, through their study of wisdom, do not wait for death to arrive, but, instead, often cast themselves onto the bonfire - this they consider to be some glorious ending. The inhabited cities here are numerous. The city of Nisa is the most famed and the largest. Mount Meros, consecrated to Jove, is held in the highest esteem by the peoples of these nations. Within one of its mountain caverns, it is supposed, certain of the gods were once nurtured, so, at least, the Greek authors have written. In this place the thigh-bone of Jove is said to have been first generated

fit:aut error.Oras tenent ab Indo ad gangem Palibotri.
a gange ad folida Nifii.ubi magis q̄ ubi habitetur:exæſtu
at:atre gentes.& quodāmodo æthiopes.Ab iolide ad eu
dum recta funt littora:timidiꝗ populi & marinis opibus
affatim dites.Tamos promontorium eſt:quodTaurus at
tollit collis alterius partis angulus initiumꝗ lateris ad me
ridiem uerſi.Ganges & Indus amnes.Ille multis fontibus
in hæmodo Indiæ monte conceptus:ſimul unum alueum
facit:fit omnium maximus & alicubi latius: quando angu
ſtiſſime fluit:decem milia paſſuum patens. In ſeptem ora
diſpergitur.Indus ex monte Paropamiſo exortus: & alia
quidem flumīa admittit. Sed clariſſima Cophē:aceſinem
Hydaſpen:conceptamque pluribus alueis undā lato ſpa
cio trahit.Hinc pene gangē magnitudine exæquat. Poſt
ubi aliquot ſæpe magnis flexibus cingit iugum ingens :
iterū rectus ſolidufque deſcendit: donec ad læuā dextráꝗ
ſe diducens duobus oſtiis longe diſtantibus exeat.ad Ta
mum inſula eſt chryſe.Ad gangem argyre. Altera aurei ſo
li:ita ueteres tradidere:altera argentei:Atꝗ ita:ut maxime
uidetur:aut ex re nomen:aut ex uocabulo fabula eſt. Ta
probane aut grandis admodū inſula: aut prima pars orbis
alterius.Hyparcho dicitur:ſed quia habitatur nec quifquā
circum eam eſſe traditur:prope uerum eſt.Contra inde il
la oſtia ſunt:quæ uocant ſolis adeo inhabitabilia:ut igreſ
ſos uis circūfuſi aeris exanimet confeſtim:& iter ipſa oſtia
rara tenet regio ob æſtus intolerabiles alicubi cultoribus
egens.Inde ad prīcipia rubri maris ptinet ipſa inuia:atque

- all of this presumes that the tales are not in error. The Palibotrians occupy the coast from the River Indus to the Ganges. From the Ganges to the headlands are the Nisians. Here the heat is intense, and the tribes are dark in the manner of the Ethiopians. From Iolis to Cudum, the coast is regular, and the people live in awe of the riches to be found off the shore. The promontory of Tamos is here, and the foothills of Mount Taurus are on the opposite side, beginning their reverse turn to the south. In this area are, first, the Ganges and, then, the Indus. From the former, many streams run from Mount Haemodus, central to all India. Beginning as a single run, it devolves into the greatest of waterways, whether running broad or narrow, even in some places ten miles wide. At its delta, it diverges into seven outlets. The Indus, however, originates from Mount Paropamisus, gathering other river as it flows. The most beautiful are the Cophes, the Acefines and the Hydaspes, each served by other streams. Together, they very nearly approach the Ganges in magnitude. This waterway, with numerous bends through the land, straightens to the place of its division into two channels, as it descends to the sea. At the promontory of Tamos is the isle of Chryse, and at the Ganges delta is the isle of Argyre. One of the isles has gold deposits, so at least the ancients held, and the other has silver. This may well be, seeing that they are named for the metal itself, or, according to the fable. The land of Taprobane is either a huge island, or the start of an unknown continent. But this much has been stated by Hyparchus: the inhabitants of the place are not accounted for, since they cannot be seen. At the far side of the place, the coast is referred to as the Uninhabited Entranceway of the Sun. Any who attempt to navigate the shore, quickly expire in the contaminated air. Between here and the river dela are scattered regions, but with few inhabitants, on account of the intolerable heat. From here to the beginning of the Red Sea is a trackless waste, and

deferta. humus cineri magis fit q̃ pulueri fimilis. Ideoq̃ p
eam rara:& non grandia flumina emanant: quorum Tu/
beronem & Arufacem noriffima accepimus. Rubrum ma
re græci fiue quia eius coloris eft. Siue quia ibi Erythras re
gnauit:Eritrhā thalaffam appellant procellofum: afperū
mare profundum & magnorum animalium magis q̃ cæ/
tera capax:primo recedentis oras æqualiter impellit. Et ut
non ītret interius aliquantum patens finus erat. Sed quas
ripas inflexerat bis irrumpit: duofque iterum finus aperit
perficus uocatur dictis regionibus propior: Arabicus ulte/
rior. Perficus qua mare accipit utrinque rectis lateribus
grande oftium quafi ceruice complectitur. Deinde terris
in omnem partem uafte & æqua portione cædentibus ma
gno littorum orbe pelagus incingens reddit formam ca
pitis humani. Arabici & os arctius & latitudo minor eft.
Maior aliquāto receffus: & multo magis longa latera init
penitus. Introrfufque dum ægyptum pene & monté ara/
biæ Cafium attingit: quodam faftigio minus:ac minus la
tus. Et quo magis penetrat anguftior. Ab iis quæ diximus:
ad finum perficum:nifi ubi chelonophagi morantur:de/
ferta funt. In ipfo Carmanii nauigantium dextra pofiti
fine uefte ac fruge:fine pecore ac fedibus. Pifcium cutæ
fe uelant. Carne uefcuntur:præter capita toto corpore hir/
futi. Interiora Cedrofi:dehinc Perfæ habitant. Cethis per
carmanios:fupra Andanis & corios effluūt. In parte quæ
pelagi oftio aduerfa eft. Babyloniorum fines chaldeorūq̃
funt:& duo clari amnes. Tigris perfidi propior. Vlterior

a desert land in which the earth resembles pulverized ash, and is similar to dust. Therefore, everything around it is sparse and spare, and no major rivers emanate from here, except for the Tuberonus and the Arusaces - this is our understanding of the matter. The Red Sea was so named by the Greeks either on account of its color, or possibly because the king Erythras reigned there, and so they called it the Red Sea (*Erythra Thalassa*). Its waters are deep and given to violent storms; it holds a multitude of giant mammals, to a greater extent than any other waterway. At the outset, its coastline recedes evenly, and unless the body is actually entered into, it would appear to be no more than an open bay. However, the waterway breaks out into two channels; the nearer of the two touches the regions of the Persian Gulf, and the further touches those of the Arabian Gulf. The Persian Gulf, at the place where it meets the ocean, spreads wide in a large inlet with curving, neck-like sides. Thereafter, the landmass, stretching all around, draws ever more narrowly toward the waters, and, at last, encompasses it in a shape that would resemble a human head. The Arabian Gulf, however, is smaller and more restricted, but the depth of its recess is somewhat greater and its interior more extended. It advances by Egypt nearly as far as Mount Casius in Arabia, at which point its breadth becomes less and less. From the things we have spoken of regarding the Gulf of Persia, everything is a barren waste, except for the area where the Chelonophagians dwell, and the land is otherwise entirely desert. But within the Gulf, the Carmanian people are seen to dwell, at the right side. They are famous as navigators. The tribes here live without clothing, grain, cattle or houses. They are covered only in the skins of fish, which is their sole sustinence. Except for the head, their bodies are hairy. At the interior of the land, is the Cedrosi tribe, with the Persians living beyond here. The River Cethis flows through the land of Carmania, as do the streams, Andanis and Corios. By the Gulf, opposite the Ocean, are the borders of the Babylonian and Chaldean people. Here, also, are two great rivers. The Tigris is close to Persia. Beyond it

Pomponii Melæ:

Euphrates. Tigris ut natus eft ita defcendens ufque ad lit
tora permeat.Euphrates immani ore aperto non exit tan
tum unde oritur:fed & uafte quoque decidit nec fecat con
tinuo agros late diffufus in ftagna diu fedentibus aquis pi
ger & fine alueo patulis.Poft ubi marginem rupit:uere flu
uius:acceptifque ripis celer & fremens per armenios & cap
padocas occidentem petit:ni taurus obftet in noftra ma
ria uenturus.Inde ad meridiem auertitur: & primum fy
ros:tum arabas ingreffus:non perdurat in pelagus:uerum
ingens modo & nauigabilis:inde tenuis riuus defpectus
emoritur:& nufquá manifefto exitu effluit: ut alii amnes
fed deficit.Alterum latus ambit plaga:quæ inter utrunque
pelagus excurrit arabia dicitur:cognomen eudæmon an
gufta uerú cinnami & thuris alioruque odorum maxime
ferax. Maiorem fabæi tenent partem oftio proximam &
carmanis contrariam partem macæ:quæ inter oftia often
ditur fyluæ cautefcqexafperant.Aliquot funt in medio in
fulæ fitæ.Ogyris qp in ea Erythræ regis monumentum eft
magis clara:q cæteræ.Alterum finum undicq arabes incin
gunt ab ea parte:quæ introeuntibus dextra eft. Vrbes funt
Carræ & arabia & gadamus. In altera ab intimo angulo.
Prima beronice inter hyeroopoliticum:& fcrobilum.De
inde inter promontoria moronenon:& colloca Philote
ris:& ptolemais ultra arfinoe:& alia beronice. Tú fylua q
hebenú odorefque generat:& manu factus amnis. Ideocq
referendus:q ex nili alueo dioryge adductus extra finú ue
rú inflexú & non rubri maris pars beftiis infefta:ideocq de

is the Euphrates. The Tigris, rising from its spring, descends directly to the shore. The Euphrates, however, rising out of a broader watershed, does not descend in so straight a manner, but, by coursing out laterally, it floods into the surrounding lands, and there, it often creates the appearance of many standing lakes, with little visible current. Finally, it overruns these basins, and, by receiving other swift tributaries, it races through Armenia and Cappadocia, lying to the west. Without the great landmass of Mount Taurus to block its path, it would almost seem to reach to our own sea. Nonetheless it turns to the south, passing first through Syria and then through Arabia. It does not follow straight to the sea, but forms a watercourse so great that it is entirely navigable. After this, it submerges below the land, and passes underground without being seen, as other rivers would be. On the opposite side is the country lying in the areas between the two gulfs which are referred to as the Arabian. This land is called Eudaemon; perhaps small in size, but rich in cinnamon, frankincense and aromatic spices. For the most part, the Sabaeans possess the part by the sea coast, but toward the land of the Carmanians, are found the Macaean people. The area between them and the coast is wooded, and difficult going. To the south is the notable isle of Ogyris, with its statue of King Erythas. The other Gulf lies around Arabia, and, on entering the waterway, Arabia is to the right. Its cities are: Carra, Arabia and Gadamus. At the upper inlet is the city of Beronice, set between the areas of Hyeropolicus and Scrobilum. Thereafter, between the promontories Moronenon and Colloca, are the cities, Philoteris and Ptolemais. Beyond is Arsinoe and the other city, Beronice. The forests of ebony trees and spices are nearby. Here is that river, made by hands, and it must be described. From the Nile, the canal was dug entirely around the Red Sea, but this land, however, is infested with wild beasts. In addition,

Liber Tertius.

ferta eft.Partem panchæi habitant hi quos ex facto: quia
ferpentibus uefcuntur ophiophagos uocant. Fuere inte
rius pygmæi minutum genus:& q; pro fatis frugibus con
tra grues dimicando defecit.Sunt multa uolucrum: mul
ta ferpentum genera. De ferpentibus memorandi maxi
me:quos paruos admodum & ueneni præfentis certo an
ni tempore ex limo concretarum paludiũ emergere in ma
gno examine uolantes ægyptum tédere:atque in ipfo in
troitu finium ab auibus. Q uas ibidas appellant: aduerfo
agmine excipi:pugnafque confici traditum eft. De uolu
cribus præcipue referenda Phœnix femper unica . Non
enim coitu concipitur partuue generatur: fed ubi quin
gentorum annorum æuo perpetuo durauit fuper exag
geratam uariis odoribus ftruem fibi ipfa incubat:foluitur
que.Deinde putrefcentium membrorum tabe concrefcés
ipfa fe concipit:atque ex fe rurfus renafcitur. Cum adole
uit offa priftini corporis inclufa myrrha ægyptum expor
tat atq; in urbem:quam folis appellant:fragrantibus nar
do buftis inferens memorando funere cófecrat.Ipfum p
montorium:quo id mare clauditur a ceraunis faltibus in
uium eft.Aethiopes ultra fedent.Meroeni habent terram
quam Nilus primo ambitu amplexus infulam facit. Pars
quia uitæ fpacium dimidio fere:q̃ nos longius agunt Ma
crobii.Pars quia ex ægypto aduenere dicti automolæ pul
chri forma & qui corporis parumque uenerariores ueluti
optimarũ alii uirtutũ.In illis mox eft cui potiffimum pa
reant fpecie ac uiribus legere:apud hos plus auri:q̃ pfis eft.

the place is a desert. In one tract live the Panchaeans, who, due to the fact that they live on serpents, are called Ophiophagians. At the interior, are the miniature Pygmies. They had once fought a battle to protect their corn lands against a flock of invading cranes, and their tribe was greatly decimated. Many such birds and serpents abound here. Noteworthy among the serpents is one small type, whose bite is fatal. They emerge, at a certain season, from the dense mud of the swamplands, and gather into great flocks to migrate to Egypt. Once there, they encounter other flocks, known as the Ibis. The Ibis fight against the intruders, and destroy them. Other birds also live there, one in particular, the Phoenix, surely the most singular of birds. Not born in the normal way - neither bred nor hatched - but only once in every five hundred years, and by nesting on a bower of aromatic spices, the bird incubates itself, and then dies. Later, out of its wasted remains, the bird conceives itself and is born anew. At adolescence, and when its bones have been wrapped in myrrh, it flies in Egypt to that city which is named for the sun (*Heliopolis*). There, it places fragrant nard, which it carries to the consecrated graves, as a funeral memorial. That promontory which forms the boundary at the shoreline, is the heavily forested Mount Ceraunis. Beyond here is the land of the Ethiopians. The Meroenians occupy that tract which is encircled by the Nile, forming there a riverine island. Some of these people appear to live half again as long as we do, and they are called the Macrobians. Other tribes, those who had once migrated from Egypt, are the Automolians. They possess beauty of face and form, and, thus, are attractive in comparison to others. Among them, it is customary to obey the most manly and virile; he is elected from within the tribe. In addition, these people possess more gold than might be found among all the Persians.

Ideo quod minus est preciosius censent.ære exornantur.
Auro uincula sonitum frabricant.Est locus apparatis epu
lis semper refertus. & quia:ut libet uesci uolétibus licet: he
liu trapezam appellant:& quæ passim apposita sunt.affir/
mant innasci subinde diuinitus.Est lacus quo perfusa cor
pora quas iuncta pernitét.Bibitur idem:adeo est liquidus
& ad sustinenda quæ incidunt aut immittuntur: infirmus
ut folia etiam proxima decisa frondibus:non innatantia
ferat sed passim & penitus accipiat.Sunt & sæuissimæ fe
ræ omni colore uarii lycaones: & quales accepimus spin/
gas.Sunt miræ aues cornutæ. Tragopomenes & equinis
auribus & Pegasi. Cæterum oras ad Eurum sequentibus
nihil memorabile occurrit.Vasta oia uastis præcisa mon/
tibus.Ripæ potius sunt:quä littora.Inde ingés & sine cul
toribus dubium aliquandiu fuit:esset ne ultra pelagus cape
ret ne terra circuitum: an exausta fructu sine fine africa se
extenderet:rerum & si Hanno carthaginensis exploratü
missus a suis.Cum per oceani ostia exisset: magnam parté
eius circunuectus:non se mari sed commeatu defecisse me
moratu rettulerat.Et Eudosus quidam auorum nostrorü
temporibus cum lathurum regem Alexandriæ profuge/
ret:arabico sinu egressus per hoc pelagus: ut nepos affir/
mat:gades usque peruectus est.Ideo eius oræ nota sunt ali
qua.Sunt autè trans ea quæ modo deserta diximus muti
populi & qbus pro eloquio nutus est.Alii siue sono liguæ
Alii sine linguis.alii labris ét co hærétibus:nisi ǫ sub nari/
bus ét fistula est:per quam bibere auent.Sed cü incessit li/

Therefore, what is less common is regarded as precious, and personal ornamentations are made of brass. Gold, instead, is made into clanking chains. There is a place for feasting, which always carries food for those who wish to dine. It is called the Table of the Sun (*Heliu Trapeza*). Anything placed upon it is considered to have come from the gods. There is a lake for bathing and for bodily refreshment; it is also used for drinking. So sheer and limpid are its waters that whatever might fall, or be thrown into it, the surface cannot sustain it; even the leaves of the trees will sink. On the other hand, wild beasts of various colors are also found here, and wolf-like creatures (*lycaones*). We understand that there are remarkable horned birds (*tragopans*), in addition to creatures with winged ears similar to horses (*pegasi*). For the remainder of the coast - even to the south-east wind (*Eurus*) - one discovers little that is memorable: vast unoccupied wastelands, broken by precipitous mountains, but streams do exist by the shore. The coast seems to be able to support a population, yet doubt had existed for long whether the sea encircled the land, or whether Africa might continue without end, out of the south wind (*ex Auster*). Hanno had once been sent out by the Carthaginians, to explore these things. He circumnavigated the greater part of the desert by the ocean, and he returned with the report that what was needed was not more sea, but more supplies. It was Eudoxus, closer to our own generation, who had once fled from King Lathurum of Alexandria. He passed through the Gulf of Arabia, even as far as our sea here. His account was later confirmed by Cornelius Nepos. The traveller had actually come to the isle of Gades. Thus, based on his tale, other things may now be stated. The areas, beyond those spoken of, would seem to be desert lands. They appear to be occupied by a people without a proper language, using, instead, signs and signals. Some lack a tongue for speech, and have a tube for air and water. Yet, when they begin to

bido uefcendi:grana fingula frugum paffim nafcentium
abforbere dicuntur.Sunt quibus ante aduentum Eudoxi
adeo ignotus ignis fuit:adeoq3 ufus mirum in modū pla
cuit:ut amplecti etiam flámas & ardentia finu abdere. Do
nec noceret maxime libuerit.Super eos grandis littoris fle
xus grandem infulam includit:in qua tantum foeminas eē
narrāt toto corpore hirfutas & fine coitu mariōn fua fpon
te foecundas adeo afperis efferifq3 moribus:ut quædā con
tineri ne reluctétur uix uinculis poffint hoc Hanno rettu-
lit:& quia detracta occifis coria pertulerat fides habita eft.
Vltra hunc finū mons altus:ut græci uocant:theon ochema perpetuis ignibus flagrat. Vltra mōtem uiret collis lō-
go tractu longis littoribus obductus.Vnde uifuntur paten
tes magis campi:quā ut profpici poffint. Panum Satyro-
rumq3 hinc opinio caufæ fidem cœpit:q3 cum in his nihil
culti fit.Nullæ habitantium fedes:nulla ueftigia: folitudo
in diem uafta.& filentium uaftius nocte crebri ignes mi-
cant:& ueluti caftra late iacentia oftenduntur.Crepāt cym
bala & tympana:audiunturq3 tibiæ fonantes maius huma
nis.Tunc rurfus æthiopes: nec iam dites: quos diximsu:
nec ita corporibus fimiles:fed minores incultique funt:&
nomine hefperio.In horum finibus fons eft:quē nili effe
aliqua credibile eft.Nuchul ab incolis dicitur.& uideri po
teft nō alio nomine appellari:fed a barbaro ore corruptius
aliter purum.& minora quidem: eiufdem tamen generis
animalia aliis omnibus in oceanum uergentibus folus in
mediam regionem ad orientem abit: & quonam exeat

eat, they are able to draw in only a single grain of corn, which grows about plentifully. So we are told. There are also those, who, before the coming of Eudoxus, did not know of fire, and they marvelled at its use. They even clasped glowing coals around their bodies, until they began to feel pain. Located above them, is a great curving body of water, holding a large island. On this isle, there are only women. It is said that they have bodily hair, and are able, without the union of marriage, to generate offspring. They have fierce ways, and some can be restrained only by chains. It was Hanno who returned with this report, and in order to overcome his detractors, he brought back the hides of some he had slain. Beyond this area, a great mountain rises up which the Greeks call *Theon Ochema* (Chariot of the Gods); well named, for its slopes blaze with perpetual fires. Another hill then arises, richly green and great in length, lying along the sea line. From it, is seen a vast plain, stretching far away. The gods, Pan and Satyr, as the opinion holds, are the reason that this tract is not cultivated, nor inhabited by people. An intense solitude is felt during the day, yet, during the night, blazing fires burst out, similar to the bonfires of an encamped army. Then, a great clash of tympani and cymbals is heard, and the cry of flutes, greater than that of any multitude. Past this place, the Ethiopians are found, but not as wealthy as the Ethiopians spoken of before. Neither are they similar in culture or bodily form. These are the Hesperian (Western) Ethiopians. In their land, however, is the fountainhead from which the Nile itself is believed to spring. The natives refer to it as Nuchul. It is not difficult to see how the name was arrived at: the barbarous speech had corrupted the more pure and shorter name. The stream generates many types of animals and beasts. It is the only river, among those flowing to the sea, which courses toward the east. With regard to the place of its initial spring,

incertum eft.Inde colligitur nilum hoc fonte conceptum
actumcz aliquandiu perinuia & ideo ignotum.iterũ fe ubi
ad ea poffit:oftendere. Cæterum fpatio quo abfconditur
effici:ut híc alio cedere:ille aliunde uideatur exurgere.Ca-
toblepas non grandis fera:uerum grande & pergrande ca
put ægre fuftinens:atcz ob id in terram plurimum ore con
uerfa:apud hos gignitur:ob uim fingularem magis etiam
referenda:cz cũ impetu morfucz nihil unquã fæuiat : ocu-
los eius:uidiffe mortiferum . Contra eofdem funt infulæ
dorcades domus:ut aiunt:aliquando Gorgonum.Ipfæ ter
ræ promontorio : cui hefperuceras nomen eft : finiuntur.
Inde incipit frons illa quæ in occidentem uergés mari atlã
tico abluitur.Prima eius æthiopes tenét.media nulli.nam
aut exufta funt:aut harenis obducta:aut in fefta ferpentibus. Exuftis infulæ appofitæ funt : quas hefperidas tenu-
iffe memoratur.In harenis mons eft fatis de fe confurgens
uerum incifis undicz rupibus præceps. inuius & quo magis furgit:exilior:qui cz altius quam confpici poteft ufcz in
nubila erigitur:cælum & fydera non tangere modo uertice fed fuftinere quocz dictus eft.Contra fortunatæ infulæ
abundant fua fpóte genitis & fubinde aliis fuper aliis inna
fcentibus nihil follicitos alunt beatius quã aliæ urbes excul
tæ.una fingulari duorum fontium ingenio maxime infi-
gnis:alterum qui guftauere rifu foluuntur in mortem . ita
affectis remedium eft ex altero bibere.Ab eo tractu qué
feræ infeftant proximi funt.Himãtopodes inflexi lentis
cruribus quos ferpere magis quã ingredi referunt.Deinde

it is uncertain. Yet, from what may be gathered, the River Nile is first generated at this fountainhead, and after some length of flowing in an unknown channel, it again openly shows its course. For another length beyond, its way is further concealed, and, on this account, some have seen it surging forth at other places, as the actual source of the springhead. The Catoblepas, while perhaps not an overly large beast, has a great - indeed, a very great - head piece upon its body; it is able to sustain itself up from the ground by it, and thereby hang upside down. The animal is widely noted for its singular strength. In addition, nothing but sudden death results from the deadly gaze of its eyes. There are certain isles nearby, the Gorgades, upon which the Gorgonians are said to have once lived. The country runs to a promontory called Hesperides, which is the land's end. From here begins that great landfront which extends to the west, and does not cease until, at last, it is washed by the Atlantic Ocean. The first part of the land here is held by the Ethiopians, but all the middle is unoccupied. The region is either consumed by heat, engulfed by sand or overrun by serpents. Desert islands lie opposite to the shore; on them, the Hesperdian tribes are still held in memory. Out of these sands, a mountain surges itself upward to a great height, sharp sided, impassable and precipitous. It would appear to rise even into the clouds and stars of heaven, almost seeming to hold them up - so it is said. Sited directly opposite to it, are those isles which are known as the Fortunates. Abundant of themselves and fruitful on their own accord, their bountiful crops grow without any solicitude of cultivation, and to an extent greater than found in any city. One of the two fountains which are there is more widely famed. Anyone who tastes of the first one, dissolves, almost to the point of expiring, with joyous laughter. Anyone who drinks of the other one, however, receives a remedy for health. But beyond here a tract of land is seen that is infested with wild beasts. Nearby are the Himatopodian people; they have bowed knees, and are forced to go about in a creep. Thereafter,

Liber Tertius.

Pharusi aliquando tendente ad hesperidas Hercule dites
nunc inculti:& nisi q pecore aluntur admodum inopes.
Hinc ia lætiores agri amœniq; saltus.Terotæ. berini ebo
re abundant.Nigritarum getuloruq; passim uagantium:
ne littora quidem in fœcunda sunt purpura:& murice ef
ficacissimis ad tingedum:& ubiq; quæ tinxere clarissima.
Reliqua est ora Mauritaniæ exterior & in finem sui fasti
giantis se africæ nouissimus angulus iisdè oppibus:sed mi
nus diues.Cæterum solo etiam ditior:& adeo fertilis est:
ut frugum genera non cum serantur modo benignissime
procreet:sed quedam profundat etiam nota. Hic Antæ
us regnasse dicitur . & signum quod fabulæ clarum pror
sus ostenditur collis modicus resupini hominis imagine
iacentis illius ut incolæ ferunt tumulus : unde ubi aliqua
pars eruta est:solent imbres spargi:& donec effossa reple
antur:eueniunt. Hominum pars syluas frequentant mi
nus q quos modo diximus uagi.Pars in urbibus habitant
quarum ut inter paruas opulentissimæ habentur procul a
mari gildano. dulbritrania. propius autem Sala & Lyxo
flumini lunxo proxima. Vltra est colonia:& fluuius gna.
& unde initium fecimus ampelusia in nostru iam fretu uer
gés promotoriu opis huius atq; atlatici littoris terminus.

Pomponii melæ Cosmographi.
Libri Tertii & Vltimi.
FINIS.

are found the Pharusian people. At one time, in the age when Hercules had gone to the kingdoms of the Hesperides, the people had been wealthy. But now they are uncultured, and, except for raising some small grazing animals, they are in poverty. Yet, now, from this place forward, we will encounter happier fields and more agreeable pastures. Both the Terotian and the Berinian tribes possess an abundance of ivory. For the Nigritians and the Getulians, even the seashore does not remain unproductive. Along their coastlands are deposits of purple and schools of murices (the shellfish). The result is a dye which can tinge any vestment to the most brilliant purple. The remainder of the seashore to Mauritania, and to the outer coast which forms the furthest headland of Africa, this same wealth is generally found. Yet some, perhaps, are not entirely so rich as those spoken of. Some soil is less productive, but elsewhere it is even more fertile, so that grain may be raised fruitfully; there are even places where it grows itself. Along here, the giant Antaeus, is said to have reigned. The sign used to demonstrate his legend is a small hill which seems to carry the image of a reclining man seen in the supine position, which the inhabitants claim to be his tomb. Should any part from this hill be dug away, a downpour of rain would fall, and would not cease until that part were again replaced. Some of the inhabitants frequent the forests, but not in the same mode as the vagabonds that we have spoken of. Some of the inhabitants live in cities, a few of which are small towns, but others live in the more wealthy cities, at some distance from the sea. They are Gildano and Dulbritrania. Closer to the sea, however, are the cities of Sala and Lyxo, these standing by the river, Lunxo. Past here is a colony, along with the river Gna. It was from this point, the mountain of Ampelusia, that we first began our work - the point where our own sea borders upon the verge of that great Promontory at the terminus of the Atlantic Ocean.

POMPONIUS MELA COSMOGRAPHER.

BOOK THREE & ULTIMATE.

THE END

Roman numerals refer to the book, and Arabic numerals refer to the page.

150

152

159

STUDIES IN CLASSICS